George Harley

The Simplification of English Spelling

Specially Adapted for the Rising Generation

George Harley

The Simplification of English Spelling
Specially Adapted for the Rising Generation

ISBN/EAN: 9783337251857

Printed in Europe, USA, Canada, Australia, Japan

Cover: Foto ©Paul-Georg Meister /pixelio.de

More available books at **www.hansebooks.com**

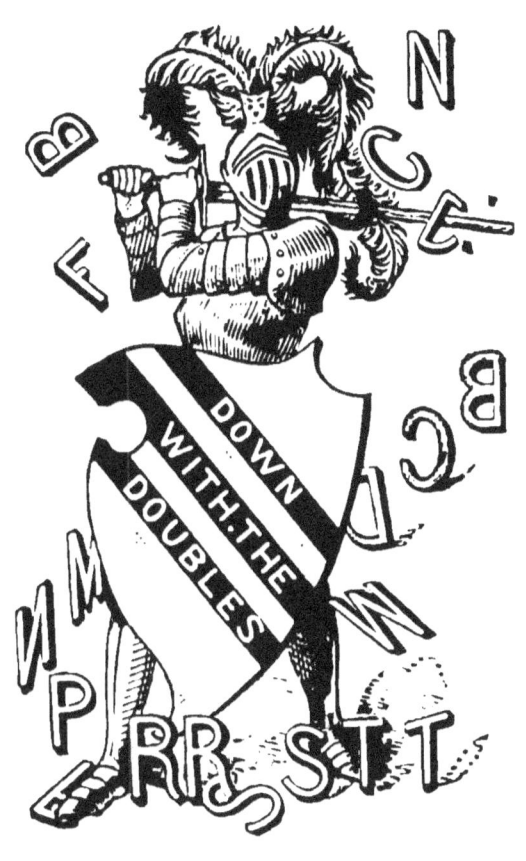

THE
SIMPLIFICATION
OF
ENGLISH SPELLING,

SPECIALLY

ADAPTED FOR THE RISING GENERATION.

An Easy Way of Saving Time

IN

WRITING, PRINTING, AND READING.

BY

Dr. GEORGE HARLEY, F.R.S., F.C.S.,

CORRESPONDING MEMBER OF THE ROYAL ACADEMY OF SCIENCES OF BAVARIA,
OF THE ACADEMY OF MEDICINE OF MADRID,
OF THE PHYSIKALISCH MEDICINISCHEN GESELLSCHAFT ZU WURTZBURG;
FORMERLY PRESIDENT OF THE PARISIAN MEDICAL SOCIETY;
AND PROFESSOR IN UNIVERSITY COLLEGE, LONDON;
ETC., ETC.

LONDON:
TRÜBNER & CO., LUDGATE HILL, E.C.

1877.

LONDON
PRINTED AT M'GOWAN AND CO.'S STEAM PRINTING WORKS,
16 GREAT WINDMILL STREET, HAYMARKET, W.

DEDICATED

TO

Anglo-Saxon Literati

OF EVERY STAMP AND SHADE,

MANY OF WHOM, LIKE MYSELF, MUST HAVE OCCASIONALLY FELT

THE MERE MANUAL PART OF LITERARY LABOR

AN IRKSOME IMPEDIMENT TO THE

EVOLUTION OF THOUGHT.

CONTENTS.

	PAGE.
Dedication	iii
On the Proposed Scheme of Spelling Reform	ix
Prolegomena	5
Number of Duplicated Consonants in a Copy of the Times	7
Difficulties in the Path of Literary Reform	8
Idiot Boy's Logic	10
Lord Palmerston's Contempt for Duplicated Consonants	13
Lord Macaulay's Use of them	14
Their Proportion; a Criterion of an Author's Literary Attainments	14
Origin of our Scheme for their Abolition	19
Etymological Difficulty Considered	19
Effect of their Omission on Pronunciation	26

Contents.

	PAGE.
The Lord's Prayer of the Twelfth Century	29
Changes in English Orthography since the Days of Queen Elizabeth	30
Diminution in the Employment of Doubled L's since then	32
The Perfection of a Language is Proportionate to the Simplicity of its Construction	33
Englishmen break the Rules of International Linguistic Etiquette	35
The Duplication of Consonants follows no Law	36
The Spelling of a Word is not necessarily an Index to its Pronunciation	41
The Pronunciation is not always an Index to its Spelling	42
Omission of Duplicated Consonants will not Induce a Change in Pronunciation	43-69
Spelling a most fallacious Test of an English Education	47
Origin and Growth of Language	48
Spelling Power Considered	52
Duplicated Consonants in Business Letters	58
Twenty Thousand Millions of Unnecessary Consonants sent Annually, in Letters alone, through the Post Office	60
Relative Proportion of Different Consonants Duplicated	61
Duplicated Consonants in Personal Names	63
A Polyglot Town	69
The Employment of Duplicated Consonants cannot be, either Philosophically or Philologically, Defended	73

Contents.

	PAGE.
Natural Linguistic Abbreviation	74
Causes Thereof	80
The Newer a Language, the Greater is its Brevity and Euphony	84
English, Scotch, French, Spanish, German, and Welsh Compared	86-96
New Phase of English Linguistic Evolution	97
General Conclusions	99
Object in Writing the Monograph	114

PRELUDE

ON THE

PROPOSED SCHEME OF SPELLING REFORM.

—◦◉◦—

The advocates of Spelling Reform, though as yet a small, are, nevertheless, a powerful band. For what they lack in number, they make up in strength.

We need only mention a few of their names to prove the truthfulness of this assertion. Among them are numbered Max Müller, A. J. Ellis, R. Morris, A. H. Sayce, E. Jones, I. Pitman, T. Pagliardini, G. Withers, and several other equally able exponents of the principles of Spelling Reform.

Already the Spelling Congress has put the machine in motion; and if it succeeds, as it anticipates, in obtaining the appointment of a Royal Commission, a most important step in the way of English Spelling Reform will be achieved.

The scheme which some of the more advanced of

our national philologists are desirous of seeing brought into operation has, unfortunately, many opponents, who ground their opposition to it on the assumption of its complexity, and, as they affirm, consequent impracticability. For the scheme not only anticipates an extensive addition to the letters in the alphabet, raising their present actual number from 26 to about 40, but, at the same time, a complete and radical change in the spelling of nearly every word in the English language.

Many persons—and we among the number—incline to the belief that if such a sweeping scheme of literary reform as is here indicated be attempted to be suddenly introduced—that is to say, before the general public is made sufficiently alive to its advantages and practicability—it will end in failure.

A Royal Commission may be appointed, and it may stamp the scheme with its official seal of approbation; but it by no means follows that the introduction of the scheme will be thereby made successful. All that a Royal Commission can do is to propose, while it entirely depends on the frame of mind of the literary classes in the nation to dispose. The majority of the educated, in a case of this kind, can alone act as arbitrators, and therefore the rejection or practical adoption of a scheme of National Spelling Reform rests entirely with them.

The Nation, we believe, may be led, but it cannot be coerced into acquiescence; and it appears to us to be a very doubtful question if the public at large are as yet at all prepared to accept of any sweeping scheme of orthographical reform.

Men of middle age shrink from the idea of having to begin and learn another, and more complex, form of alphabet. They tremble at the very thought of having to commence a course of spelling anew. They even, to a certain extent, dread the prospect of having their visual organs offended by the abnormal appearance which a new form of words is likely to present.

These objections, though they may appear trifling when looked at individually, will nevertheless, we fear, be ascertained to be formidable obstructive agents in the way of orthographical reform when they exert their influence collectively.

Let them be eradicated from the public mind, and the path to Spelling Reform would at once be open.

Now comes the question,—How is this desirable object to be attained?

Simply, we believe, by educating the public mind to perceive THE WANT OF THE PERIOD, and opening its eyes to the practicability of the scheme of reform.

1st. John Bull being essentially an L. S. D. gentleman, must, at the very outset, have it clearly demonstrated to his mind that the adoption of the scheme of reform proposed to him will be to his pecuniary advantage.

2nd. As John Bull does not enjoy the prospect either of trouble or inconvenience being entailed upon him, the second thing is to prove to his satisfaction that the practical adoption of the scheme would not cause him much personal inconvenience.

3rd. If, in addition to these two points, it could be incontrovertibly shown to him that the introduction of a system of reformed spelling would not only be a national benefit, but, at the same time, a personal convenience to every man, woman, and child in the realm, he would soon cease to oppose the reform movement.

4th. Taking these three propositions as granted, the next step is to consider—How best his education in Spelling Reform can be conducted?

We are of opinion that the public mind can be most readily brought to see the advantages of Spelling Reform, not by furnishing it with a quantity of learned books on philology, but by entertaining it with a few treatises, giving a popular explanation of the subject: and we imagine that as its eyes become opened, its prejudices will in a corresponding proportion diminish, until at last they entirely disappear.

Like most other men, we form theories; and on the subject of Spelling Reform we have a theory. It is, that John Bull cannot be successfully dealt with by attempting to take him by the horns, but that he may be overcome by appealing to his reason.

We are still further of opinion that when an individual, or a class of individuals, cannot readily obtain all at once what he wants, the best plan for him to adopt is to direct his energies to the attaining of the object piecemeal.

A new alphabet and new phonetic spelling appears to us too large a mouthful to be forced upon the nation all at once. It would be better, we think, to try and give it such a huge lump broken up in small pieces. With this object in view, we beg to propose the following plan of procedure, which, although it may take some years to complete, has, at least, the great advantage of causing a minimum of national inconvenience, while the mere loss of the few years in point of time which it necessitates, is, in a matter of this kind, of mere secondary importance to the nation.

Our scheme is this :—

1st. Let us begin by following the natural course of linguistic evolution, and at once omit all duplicated consonants from English words, not one of which, as we shall afterwards show in this monograph, is absolutely necessary. Duplicated vowels, on the other hand, must not be interfered with, as they are an essential index to pronunciation. But doubled b's, c's, d's, f's, g's, h's, &c., are totally unnecessary. So we would propose to do entirely away with them, except in personal names, for reasons to be given afterwards at page 63.

2nd. After duplicated consonants have been satisfactorily expunged from English literature (with the advantage of having thereby a great number of words abbreviated), we propose that the next step—still following in the normal course of linguistic evolution—should be to omit from every word in the English language all mute letters of the alphabet—vowels, as wells as consonants. Thus Isle, we would write Ile, and Island, Iland. Which would again induce a still further abbreviation in a multitude of words.

3rd. The eye having thus become familiarised with the changed appearance of words, and the hand habituated to the change in their orthography, we should again advance a step further—to the climax of Spelling Reform—and now proceed to spell and write phonetically.

A little reflection will, we think, prove that the *ultima thule* of Spelling Reform is much more likely to be reached in this way, by progressive stages, than by one sudden, fell, literary swoop.

Moreover, our plan of Spelling Reform has the following nine advantages, each individual one of which has a special practical importance of its own.

A. The omission of duplicated consonants necessitates no re-education whatever.

B. The dropping out of mute letters from words can be readily done by the least learned members of the community.

C. The omission of letters will entail no mental effort upon anyone, after a day or two's practice.

D. It will at once lead to a considerable saving of Time and Labour in Writing, Printing, and Reading.

E. It will diminish expense, by saving, not only time, but materials. Paper, pens, type, and ink will be saved.

F. This scheme of omitting letters can easily proceed side by side, and hand-in-hand, with the present methods of writing and printing, which a few ultra-conservative members of society may prefer to adhere to.

G. The omission of certain letters from words will not in any way interfere with the value of existing libraries and literature, which, most unfortunately, the adoption of the Congress meditated scheme of Reform will inevitably do.

H. It offers a personal advantage to every man, woman, and child in the nation, and will be an equal boon to the Lazy, as well as to the Busy, members of the community.

I. Finally, the general adoption of our scheme would be a most advantageous stepping-stone to the practical introduction of the grand scheme meditated by the Spelling Reform Congress, to which we most heartily wish success.

It may not be out of place for us here to remark, that this little monograph is merely intended to advocate our own personal opinions on Spelling Reform, in so far as the first stage of our scheme is concerned. For we think, that in this instance, at least, it will be found, as the French say, "ce n'est que le premier pas qui coute," and that once the first stage has been successfully got over, the others will follow as a natural sequence in the chain of linguistic continuity. The book is not written in an abstruse, but in a popular manner, as it was originally put in type solely for the purpose of private distribution among our personal friends, many of whom take an interest in the subject. Some of them having, however, suggested to us the desirability of giving to our views a more extended circulation, a few extra copies have been placed in the hands of Mr. Trübner, for disposal to the general public. There is a slight difference in the private copies; but it is one of a very trifling character.

25 HARLEY STREET, W.,
June, 1877.

PROLOGOMENA.

"TO THE PEN, AND THE PRESS, WE POOR MORTALS OWE
MUCH THAT WE HAVE, AND NEARLY ALL THAT WE KNOW."

AS there exists a Philosophy in Language, as well as in pure Science, we purpose to discuss the question of the Simplification of English Spelling, according to the system of the Aristotelian school.

Each independent fact to be adduced in the chain of evidence will therefore be separately submitted to consideration, weighed, and appraised on its own individual merits, and from the whole collective data the general conclusion will at last be drawn.

In thus applying the inductive method of philosophy to the subject now before us, it will not be to the imaginative; but to the reasoning faculties alone, that we shall appeal for our reader's support.

None but those who have already given special attention to the important part played by consonants in English literature can possibly suppose that the topic of this essay is not only one of national importance, but at the same time one actually involving the personal convenience of every man, woman, and child reading and writing the English language.

Even editors and publishers, as a rule, possess nothing beyond a very vague idea of the extent to which consonants are employed in daily literary routine.

It will even surprise the uninitiated to learn that they labor under a delusion in thinking that the present mode of employing doubled b's, c's, d's, f's, g's, l's, &c., is productive of only trifling public inconvenience. But the sequel of this essay will, in all probability, emancipate them from this pleasing delusion, as well as also prove to them that the evil, though great, is, nevertheless, easily remediable.

The number of doubled d's, f's, m's, t's, s's, &c., which infest English literature is far beyond the power of human calculation. A glance at the *Times* newspaper will suffice to illustrate the truthfulness of this assertion.

Few persons, we imagine, are aware that each full-sized copy of the newspaper which they so gladly welcome to their breakfast-table in the morning contains more than thirty thousand doubled b's, c's, d's, f's, g's, &c., and that it daily entails upon their visual organs the necessity of deciphering exactly one half—that is to say, more than fifteen thousand —absolutely unnecessary letters of the alphabet, which not only take up a quantity of valuable space in the journal, but must have consumed much valuable time both in their writing and in their printing, besides giving rise to other disadvantages, which need not be here specially alluded to.

Moreover, if every daily copy of the *Times* newspaper was equally full-sized, instead of sometimes consisting of twelve instead of sixteen pages, it would compel its readers to peruse no fewer than four millions seven hundred and fifty-three thousand unnecessary letters of the alphabet in the space of every year. The *Times*, too, be it remembered, is not peculiar in this matter. All newspapers, journals, books, as well as business and social letters of correspondence yield a full quota of unnecessary consonants. So that the annual production of unnecessary consonants in English literature must be computed by millions upon millions of millions.

Fortified with this knowledge, no one will surely venture to assert that the discussion of the subject now before us is one of trivial importance to the community.

In introducing our subject, it may be advisable to remark that we are in no degree blind to the difficulties which beset the path to literary reform. We are quite cognisant of the fact that there are at least two formidable obstacles in the way,

PREJUDICE AND HABIT.

Familiarity, the great breeder of contempt, induces every one to treat with indifference the existence of inconsistencies in his mother tongue, which, were they for the first time brought under his notice after his intellectual faculties had become developed, would fret, jar, and annoy him to such an extent, that they would at once be unhesitatingly discarded as intolerable.

The human mind tardily appreciates advantages likely to arise from working in other grooves from those in which it has become habituated to labor.

All men are slaves to habit, quite as much as they are slaves to prejudice, and we believe that it will be more on account of the passive resistance of these twin sisters than anything else that the plan of improving our spelling, and thereby saving both time and labor now about to be explained will encounter a difficulty in being adopted. We, therefore, earnestly plead on its behalf a calm and impartial hearing ere it is subjected to adverse criticism. Before judgment is pronounced against it, let its case, at least, have the benefit of careful consideration. Flaws in the brief, we doubt not there are, but the flaws we believe are entirely due, not to the weakness of the case, but to the want of skill in its advocate.

It was once said by a wiseacre that the majority of men are fools, and if the minor half only got the chance, it would lock up the major half of its fellow men in a madhouse. Be this true, or be it false, there is no doubt whatever that many of the actions of perfectly sane men possess in them a strong inter-mixture of folly. The inveterate force of habit is of itself a proof of this. Our actions are often contrary to our reason; and no more graphic illustration of the innate tendency to folly of the human mind can be given than by citing the case of a poor idiot lad, who, on being asked by a kind-hearted old gentleman why he was so very lame, gave the prompt reply, " A hae a nail in the heel of ma bute" (I have a nail in the heel of my boot). "Why don't you pull it out, then?" the gentleman retorted. "O! cause a'm yeused wi'd" (Oh! because I am used to it), was the sage reply. Now, although this was but the logic of a poor idiot boy, humiliating though the fact be, it nevertheless illustrates to a nicety the principle upon which the vast majority of mankind act throughout life; and the most formidable obstacle to the removal of the evil of duplicated consonants from our language will probably be, that like the nail in the heel of the boy's boot, "we're yeused wi'd."

It must not be forgotten that no 'human' law is immutable. That everything earthly is in a perpetual state of change, from the ever restless ambient air to the apparently stolid adamantine rock.

Science tells us that with every tick of the clock myriads of atoms—inorganic as well as organic—dead as well as living—continually and uninterruptedly "ring the changes," although their transition movements are imperceptible to the human eye.

Philology, in like manner, tells us that year by year, week by week, all languages are perpetually passing through states of change—many old words gradually becoming obsolete, while of new there is a continuous accession.

The pronunciation, too, of one and the same word gradually becomes altered. Its spelling varies, its meaning changes from generation to generation, though, as in the physical world, the process of the philological transition is equally unappreciable to the human perception until the change has actually become *un fait accompli*.

Fortunately for us, the changes now induced year by year in the Anglo-Saxon language are of a decidedly progressive, and not retrogressive character, so that no attempt need be made to stem their onward current.

Fate, the immediary* law-giver and austere judge of the universe, is shown in the essay to have donned the black cap and passed sentence of death on many of the senile incongruities which infest the English language, more particularly upon all Duplicated-Consonants and

* Word coined from immediacy.

unnecessary vowels, and "Old Father Time" is indicated as their appointed executioner.

Still further, we think that in the subsequent pages it is conclusively shown that, although his labors are slow, they are nevertheless as inevitable as they are relentless, and illustrate well the old Italian proverb, "*Chi va piano va sano.*"

Moreover, we imagine that it is not only undeniably proved that all Duplicated-Consonants are capable of a speedy removal without a single inconvenience besetting the path, but that, at the same time, an immediate, as well as a permanent, benefit will accrue to all kinds of English literature by their abolition.

The fact of an "Evil" possessing a hoary head is no valid excuse for its perpetuation, and above all things, the perpetuation of an evil in language is totally inexcusable; seeing that language is in its very nature as unstable as the ocean—ever on the ebb or flow.

Should even nothing more be gained by this exposition than a tacit acknowledgment that all duplicated-consonants are inevitably doomed to disappear from the English language, an important point will have been achieved. For with this patent fact before their eyes, persons will soon cease to fear that the occasional dropping out of a doubled consonant from a word can be regarded as a sign of an inferior education, while the total omission of them from a written document will, on the other hand, gradually come to be viewed in the light of a proof of an advanced education.

Strange to say, some of the greatest intellects of our times have an utter contempt for the employment of duplicated consonants, and we might quote several; but not desiring to appear invidious, we shall refrain from citing the names of living celebrities, and limit ourselves to adducing that of the late Lord Palmerston as a striking example of the truthfulness of this remark. In corroboration of this statement we may mention that there hangs at this moment—or did hang, at least a few years ago—over the chimney-piece of the coffee-room of the George Hotel, at Bangor, a framed letter from Lord Palmerston, in which he, the then Premier of England, praises the accommodation afforded by the inn, spelling the word "inn" with a single "n."

Moreover, we have discovered, by calculation, that the higher the literary style of an author, the fewer are the words with duplicated consonants which he employs.

Compare, for example, the high class writing of Lord Macaulay's ' Critical and Historical Essays" with the humdrum style of a third-class novelist, and it will soon become apparent on which side the greatest abundance of duplicated consonants are to be found.

One does not need even to go so far as this, for a glance at any newspaper will prove the fact.

Every newspaper contains at least three well-marked styles of literary composition—a first, a second, and a third-rate style. The first class may be said to comprise the leading articles ; the second class to be the product of the pen of the so-called penny-a-liner ; and the third class the florid style of the puffing trade advertiser.

By comparing the number of duplicated-consonants in the writings of these different classes, including those in proper names, it will be found that the smallest ratio is met with in the leading articles, the highest in the advertisement columns, and the medium in the ordinary paragraphs ; so that we are thus furnished with the curious fact, that the ratio of duplicated-consonants in a literary production is to a certain extent a criterion of the author's literary power. From a calculation founded on the examination of more than fifty thousand words selected from different writings, the standard of good class writing appears to be represented by the ratio of one word in every fifteen, containing a duplicated-consonant. A smaller proportion of words with duplicated consonants, *cæteris paribus*, indicating a superior, while a larger proportion of duplicated-consonants denotes an inferior order of English composition.

After placing these facts before the mind's eye, it is endeavoured to be shown that, no matter however reluctant one may at first feel to share in the downfall of an old custom, it ought, notwithstanding, to be impossible for any enlightened person to hesitate long before lending a helping hand in the removal from the path of literature of a number of effete obstacles; seeing that, while on the one hand, their ultimate overthrow is absolutely unavoidable; on the other, their speedy demise will be accompanied by an immediate and unsullied advantage to every educated Anglo-Saxon.

With these, not unnecessary, preliminary remarks we shall now enter upon the proper consideration of our subject.

SIMPLIFICATION.

EVERY century, every age, is known to manifest some special peculiarity, and the nineteenth century and the present age offers no exception to this rule.

If we glance around us on the fields of agriculture, mechanics, art, or science, we everywhere encounter the same prominent symptom, the symptom of "Simplification." The mowing machine is employed because it reaps in the brief space of an hour more corn than a laborer can cull in a whole day. Steam is applied to purposes of locomotion, to enable us to travel between dusk and dawn a greater distance than could formerly be accomplished within a week. The art of the photographer again enables mere manual skill to develope in a few minutes a more exact likeness than an accecomplished miniature painter can pourtray in as many hours. By the simplification of scientific principles we are enabled to waft ideas across the broad Atlantic in the twinkling of an eye, which in former years failed to be transmitted to the same distance within a month.

Let us, indeed, gaze on what side we may, the process of philosophic Simplification ever seems to be in the ascendant. It curtails labor, it saves time, it engenders speed, and as time is said to be synonymous with money, Simplification may be regarded as the synonym of profit.

Literature alone hangs fire in the general reform movement.

Our methods of communicating ideas by the intervention of paper and ink are but little easier now than they were three hundred years ago.

Many reforms are urgently required in this age of speed to facilitate the inter-communication of thought. He must be a slow-brained author whose ideas are not generated in his mind a vast deal quicker than his pen can pourtray them, and he must be an unusually easy-going individual who does not feel the mere manual part of literary labor an almost intolerable incubus on his work.

It is difficult to indicate the precise shape which reforms in literary labor may henceforth assume; but at the present moment there is at least one which can easily be delineated, and it is with it alone that we purpose now to deal.

Everyone knows that great dissatisfaction, almost universally, exists among the thinking part of educated Anglo-Saxons regarding the inconsistencies in the orthography of their language, and various have been the plans at different times suggested with the view of remedying the defect. Hitherto, however, none of the suggested plans have met with general approval. The various plans appear to have failed in their object from two principal causes.

Firstly, the majority of the propositions embodied in them have been too sweeping, and too complicated in their character to admit of easy introduction. Secondly, the *laissez aller* nature of the human mind is a formidable stumbling-block in the way of any improvement, be its object what it may.

The scheme of simplifying English literature now suggested is, fortunately, entirely devoid of this first class of objections, while at the same time it will probably ingratiate itself with the majority of persons from the welcome fact that it proposes a saving of labor, and consequently a saving of time—a saving of labor and a saving of time being a boon alike to the lazy as well as to the busy members of the community.

The plan owes its origin to the following circumstances. In the early part of our University career, a book published in the sixteenth century was placed in our hands, and during its perusal surprise was felt that it contained a number of words spelt with duplicated consonants which are at the present time spelt only with single ones. This not unnaturally gave birth to the question :—

"IF SO MANY DUPLICATED CONSONANTS HAVE BEEN EXPUNGED WITH APPARENT ADVANTAGE, WHY ARE ANY RETAINED AT ALL?"

To this seemingly simple query no satisfactory reply presented itself, although at first sight it appeared probable that duplicated consonants were retained in compound words, on philological grounds, in order to enable their etymology to be readily traced. This reason was, however, rapidly abandoned, as glaring instances presented themselves, where in some of the most simple compound words the original formation of the word has been entirely disregarded. Take, for example, the simple word welcome. Who would now think of spelling it with two l's? No one. The only occasion, indeed, in which we ever remember to have seen it so written, was when Queen Victoria visited Paris. It then appeared on a triumphal arch on the Boulevard des Italiens as "Wellcome Victoria," the literal translation of *bien venu*.*

An equally palpable contradiction is met with in the word matter, which, when compounded into materialism, is robbed of a t. Then, again, exactly the same thing has occurred with our sacred word Almighty (all powerful), which, etymologically written, would be Allmighty. Yet no one now-a-days ever dreams of so penning it.

Although there is no fear that the enlightened philologist will cavil with the proposed abolition of duplicated consonants on etymological grounds—as it is possible that the majority of our readers, who are less learned in the science, may attach an unnecessary amount of importance to the value of duplicated consonants in tracing the etymology of words, by attaching subtle reasons to the causes of things

* Thom Speed, in his large and learned work on the "Theatre of the Empire of Great Britain," published in 1611, notwithstanding his fondness for double l's (as will afterwards be shown) spelt well with only one l, as wel.

where none actually exist, except in their own imagination—we think it desirable specifically to call their attention to the following facts :—

1st. The etymology of words is traced by phonetic similarity.

2nd. All letters of the alphabet nearly phonetically alike are transmutable into each other without offering the slightest impediment to etymological research.

3rd. In no case whatever does the tracing correctly the etymology of a word entirely depend on the presence or absence of a duplicated letter.

Illustrative of these three propositions, we may cite the changes which the common word father has undergone, in its journey towards us and other European languages, from the original Sanskrit word

PITAR.

Teutonic, Fader.	Greek, Πατηρ.
Modern German, Vater.	Latin, Pater.
Anglo-Saxon, Fadeur.	Italian, Padre.
Modern English, Father.	French, Père.

It is here seen that, notwithstanding the very marked transmutations which have occurred with the original word pitar, in adopting it into the modern languages of Europe, there is yet no philological difficulty experienced in tracing the various words now used by the different nationalties back to their original root. It would, therefore, be puerile to say that the mere leaving out of a consonant, where two similar ones come together, would in the slightest degree interfere with the studies of the scientific philologist. We shall even proceed a step further, and show that even in modern times, and among the most learned men of the nation, a total disregard is still paid to literal etymological spelling, both in the adoption of foreign words, and in the construction out of them of compound words adopted from foreign languages—and this, too, without giving occasion to the slightest etymological inconvenience.

For example, the words tonsil and spleen are the technical English words for two organs in the animal body, the former word being derived from the irregular p¹ ural Latin noun tonsillæ, the latter from the singular Greek noun σπλην (splen); and in adopting these words into the English language the original spelling of each has been changed, by lopping off an l from the one, and by adding an e to the other. The precise reason for thus lengthening the one word and shortening the other is not quite patent to the mental eye, and still less intelligible is the reason why when, after this change had been actually made, as soon as the words were compounded with 'itis,' denoting inflammation, the lopping off and lengthening process was again had recourse to: but in exactly the reverse manner. The results being the formation of the compound words tonsillitis, with two l's, and splenitis, with one e.

If this second change was made on etymological grounds, with the view of restoring the English derivatives to their originals before transforming them into compound words, the object of the measure remains equally obscure, seeing that their etymology was utterly ignored in the first instance, when they were converted into English words. After dropping an l out of the one and adding an e to the other, and thus, as it were, stamping them as new English words, there was no valid philological necessity for again having recourse to lopping out an e and adding an l in order to restore the words to their original spellings before compounding them.*

---

* The 'e' in the Greek 'splen' is long, but that is no reason for writing two 'e's' in spleen, and a single one only in 'splenitis.'

The same etymological reason which held good in the latter, ought surely, with equal force, to have held good in the former case.

It will be observed, too, that the true clue to the etymology of the words in question does not, in the least degree, depend either on the presence of an additional l in the one, or the absence of a double c in the other. Moreover, an hybridism is here seen to have offered no impediment to the construction of the compound word.

In Speed's "Empire of Great Britain" such monosyllabic words as son, won, sin, map, lap, stem, and war, are not only spelt with duplicated consonants, but with an additional e at the end of each of them. Thus they are written—sonne, wonne, sinne, mappe, lappe, and warre; and one might, perhaps, be excused asking the question, Whether it is the old or the new form of spelling which is founded on the best philological principles?

In fact, the presence or absence of duplicated consonants has little or nothing to do with the true etymological understanding of any language; therefore, their total abolition from the English language cannot be objected to on purely etymological grounds, except by those super-acute-minded individuals who are in the habit of "discovering subtle intentions in the shallow felicities of chance."

The next reason which occurred to our minds against the abolition of duplicated consonants was the probability of it leading to inextricable confusion by entailing upon us the necessity of spelling alike words with entirely different significations. Thus hoping and hopping, riding and ridding, along with a number of other words, would be thereby rendered orthographically undistinguishable from each other. A very moderate amount of acumen, however, and the use of a dictionary by those who have defective memories, will soon prove the contrary. The beautiful and logical English language already contains within its borders a whole legion of words with entirely different significations, yet possessing identical spellings. Here is subjoined a few of them :—

Yard, an enclosure.   Yard, a measure.
Fold, a sheep-pen.   Fold, to double up.
Skate, a fish.   Skate, to slide on ice.
Sole, a fish.   Sole, the bottom of a boot.
Punch, an iron tool.   Punch, whisky toddy.
Bay, a colour.   Bay, an indentation of coast.
Draught, a drink.   Draught, the act of drawing.
Gum, part of the mouth.   Gum, an exudation from a tree.
Slight, thin.   Slight, an insult.
Custom, a tax.   Custom, a habit.
Well, healthy.   Well, a fountain.

Porter, a man.	Porter, a drink.
Tender, sensitive.	Tender, coal-truck attached to an engine.
Lie, a falsehood.	Lie, to recline.
Bear, an animal.	Bear, to carry.
Weal, prosperity.	Weal, mark of a whip.
Plan, a design.	Plan, to invent.
Plant, a vegetable.	Plant, to fix.
Bow, the stem of a boat.	Bow, to bend.
Low, opposite of high.	Low, to bellow like an ox.
Cruise, a small cup.	Cruise, to sail in a ship.

Many more examples of this kind might be cited: but these are surely sufficient to convince any ordinarily constituted mind that there exists but little risk of causing confusion by dropping out duplicated consonants, and thereby slightly adding to the number of words with different meanings which already exist in the language spelt alike.

As must readily be seen, it is not the mere word, *per se*, but the context which is the true index of its meaning. To this important point we shall again take occasion to refer, and that, too, with greater force.

Another reason against the abolition of duplicated consonants which presented itself was the possibility of its leading the ignorant to pronounce all words alike which are spelt similarly.

This argument, like its predecessors, totally

failed to stand the test of close scrutiny. A little reflection revealed the existence of a host of words which, although spelt alike, are, nevertheless, pronounced differently. This statement looks very like a philological improbability, yet a glance at the subjoined list of words will soon prove it to be an orthographical fact. Thus we have—

Bow, a weapon to shoot with.	Bow, to bend.
Essay, a composition.	Essay, to analyse.
Minute, small.	Minute, a period.
Sow, a pig.	Sow, to sow seed.
Resign, to yield up.	Resign, to sign again.
Bass, lowest notes in music.	Bass, a mat.
Divers, different.	Divers, persons who dive.
Does, the plural of doe.	Does, third person singular of do.
Polish, belonging to Poland.	Polish, to brighten.
Tarry, covered with tar.	Tarry, to linger.
Conjure, to juggle.	Conjure, to entreat.
Entrance, a doorway.	Entrance, to charm.
August, a month.	August, great.
Refuse, rubbish.	Refuse, to decline.
Row, a tumult.	Row, to propel a boat.
Close, a confined space.	Close, to shut.
Excuse, an apology.	Excuse, to pardon.
House, a dwelling.	House, to lodge.
Noose, a slip knot.	Noose, to catch.
Invalid, a sick person.	Invalid, not valid.
Put, a game at cards.	Put, to throw a stone, to place.
Tear, a drop from the eye.	Tear, to rend asunder.
Incense, church scent.	Incense, to irritate.
Frequent, often.	Frequent, to visit.
Subject, a thing.	Subject, to compel.

Object, a thing.	Object, to refuse.
Gout, a disease.	Gout, taste.
Desert, a wilderness.	Desert, what one merits.
Lead, a metal.	Lead, to conduct.
Sewer, a plaintiff.	Sewer, a drain.
Wind, air in motion.	Wind, to twist.
Bound, tied.	Bound, to jump.

And many, many more such examples could be adduced in support of the assertion did it seem necessary to do so, but there can be little doubt this list will be deemed more than ample.

It will be seen, too, that in craving for the abolition of duplicated consonants we are not seeking to do a thing that will make the language one whit less logical than it already is. On the contrary, we dare venture to opine that, were every duplicated consonant swept from it to-morrow, the language would be more simple, more logical, and more beautiful—easier for our children to learn, easier for ourselves to write, and much less troublesome to our foreign friends. Moreover, in thus desiring the abolition of duplicated consonants, strange to say, we are but seconding the efforts, and seeking to shorten the labors, of "Old Father Time;" for he, after his own peculiar fashion, has, during the last three centuries, been slowly, but surely, doing the very thing which we are anxious to do. This statement is easily proved.

Look at English spelling in times gone by, and it will be seen that many, very many, of the words which were formerly spelt with duplicated consonants are now written with only single ones. It will be quite unnecessary for us to go back to early Anglo-Saxon literature in order to illustrate this point; indeed, were we to attempt to do so we should find it a very difficult task, as there are too few of the original Anglo-Saxon words left which bear a sufficient resemblance to those now in daily use to enable us to make an exact orthographical standard of comparison between them. Old Anglo-Saxon reads much more like a foreign language than anything else. Thus the Lord's Prayer of the twelfth century is, "Fadeur, ur in heune, haleweide beith thi neune, simin thi kuneriche, thi wille beoth idon in heune and in erthe. The euryen dawe bried, gif ous thilk dawe. And vorrgif ure dettes as vi vorrgifen ure dettoures. And lene us nought into temtation, bot delyvor eus of evel. Amen." A.D. 1158.*

In truth, the whole of King Alfred's English (1,000 years ago) is totally unintelligible to all English scholars, except the few who have made it a special study; and the English of

* Diprose's Annual, p. 108.

the present day will probably be as incomprehensible to our successors of 1,000 years hereafter, as that of King Alfred is to us now. No doubt the future changes in our language will be fewer in quantity and slower in quality than those of the past, as there are now powerful conservative forces at work which were not before in existence. These we shall point out further on; for our purpose it is only requisite to include in our review what is commonly called Modern English—that is to say, the language which has been employed since the advent of Caxton and his printing press; the introduction of Protestantism, and the more general diffusion of literature among the laity (which began in the sixteenth century), by which it has been supposed that the language acquired a sufficiently complete organisation to merit the title of Modern English.

To indicate a few of the changes which consonants have undergone in their employment since the days of Queen Elizabeth will be, therefore, sufficient for our purpose, and by thus avoiding pressing into our service ancient English, we shall probably prevent adverse criticism from cavillers, over the early construction of the language.

In a letter addressed to Queen Elizabeth by

Sir Martin Frobisher, and published in his "Arctic Voyages," he writes "that he had been shott in the legg with a bullett;" but who among us would spell shot and bullet with two t's, or leg with two g's.

At the very moment this paper is being revised, there lies on the table before us the March number of the *Leisure Hour* (1876), and at page 132 there is a copy of a letter from the Rev. J. Ellis, dated 26th Oct., 1673, in which he spells sap—sappe, permit—permitt, and let—lett.

Innumerable other examples might be cited of the unnecessary frequency of duplicated consonants in the writings of the seventeenth and eighteenth centuries; but every one must be so perfectly familiar with this fact that there can be no necessity for quoting more.

Many of the present generation will remember that when at school they were taught to spell waggon with two g's, while it is now spelt with only one g. Fulfil, skilful, and wilful, each with four l's, and dulness with two. Now, however, each of these words has had its l's diminished to one-half. The diminution, too, came about gradually; first, only one of the l's was quietly dropped out, and we had fulfill, skilfull, and wilfull—and, as is seen, without any regard being paid to the order in which the diminution of the l's was made—then, after a short time more had elapsed, "Time," the executioner, again stepped in with his pruning-hook, and silently cut off the third l; so that the words are now reduced to fulfil, skilful, and wilful.

The writings of the seventeenth century abound in double l's. If, for example, we look at "His Pilgrimage," by Purchas, we shall find that he writes equall, jewell, marvell, metall, and naturall; or, at Speed's "Theatre of Great Britain" (1611), we shall find the words admirall, generall, loyall, royall, quarell, actuall, eternall, imperiall, prodigall, gospell, poeticall, cattell, minerall, and counsell—all of which words have been robbed of the double l without a single voice having been raised against the innovation; the whole Anglo-Saxon world having quietly acquiesced in the change, and if we are not mistaken, even regarded it with something akin to approbation.

Why then should we be reluctant to proceed a step further, and abolish all double l's?

The gradual and slow, yet sure, shortening of English words may be illustrated yet in another way. If we look at a series of dictionaries in chronological order, it will be found, we believe, that they present marked differences in the spelling of identical words. Thus: —

  Cotgrave's Dictionary published Circa. 1650.
  Johnson's ,, ,, ,, 1750.
  Webster's ,, ,, ,, 1850.
In the first, music and frolic are spelt, musicke and frolicke.
 ,, second ,, ,, musick and frolick.
 ,, third ,, ,, music and frolic.

Each succeeding century amputated a letter from each of the words, and yet, after the operation, the one remained as full of melody, and the other as brimful of fun as ever. So it is seen that, without any attending discomfort, the words have been made less troublesome, alike to the writer and to the reader, and the language itself has been a gainer thereby; every step towards Simplification being a step towards perfection.

The perfection of a machine consists, in a great measure, in the simplicity of its construction. In like manner,

THE PERFECTION OF A LANGUAGE CONSISTS IN THE SIMPLICITY OF ITS CONSTRUCTION.

The more ideas that can be expressed in the smallest number of words, and the shorter the words are in which they can be expressed, the more simple, the more perfect, and, consequently, the more beautiful is the language.

Let us glance for a moment at our less fortunate German friends, and see what circumlocution they are compelled to adopt in order to express themselves correctly.

Some of their scientific words fill nearly whole lines; some of their scientific sentences occupy nearly whole pages. This is a slight exaggeration, but only very slight.

Many years ago, when talking on this subject, we were challenged by a friend to adduce a single instance written by the late Baron von Liebig that contained more than fifty words. Rising from the table, we went into the study, and returned with a printed address of his to the Academy of Sciences of Bavaria, which had arrived from him that very morning. A very short search discovered a sentence which contained over one hundred and fifty words. And Baron Liebig, be it remembered, was not a bad scientific German writer.

But to return to Duplicated-Consonants. Our German friends spell man with two n's; and it may be asked if their mann is any more of a man than ours? Again, our French friends spell their "appartements" with two p's; but does that make them the smallest bit more comfortable than ours? No, not a whit.

The spelling is here a mere matter of choice. It is rather strange, too, that both words—man and apartment—are taken by us from these respective nations; and yet we did not hesitate to drop from them the duplicated-consonants, even without their consent.

IT IS NOT ALONE IN THE MODE OF ADOPTING ORDINARY WORDS FROM FOREIGN LANGUAGES THAT ENGLISHMEN BREAK THE RULES OF INTERNATIONAL ETIQUETTE.

We are unfortunately guilty of a far greater crime in changing altogether the spelling of the proper names of foreign towns. Thus we have for no tangible reason whatever transformed Venezia into Venice, Wien into Vienna, and Munchen into Munich, without apparently the slightest compunctions of conscience. Nay, more: we daily permit our explorers to alter entirely the native names of places, and they very often substitute a vastly inferior-sounding title for a euphonious one. It is said that a barbaric Briton has transformed the sweet-sounding native name Kalinda—a beautiful ravine in one of our colonies—into the harsh-sounding title of Dick's Gully, or something like that. Verily,

A LAW MIGHT BE PASSED WITH ADVANTAGE TO RESTRAIN OUR NATIONAL CONCEIT FROM GIVING NEW NAMES TO FOREIGN PLACES.

For it frequently leads to great difficulty in identifying the place, from its new name being totally different from its ancient native title.

Moreover, persons ought to be restrained from giving to places already possessing native names, others that have been previously elsewhere appropriated, and thereby engendering geographical ambiguity.

Between England, America, and Australia there are already no less than three different towns named London, four called Portsmouth, six Newcastle, and seven Richmond. Our Teutonic brethren have gone still further, and succeeded in dotting the world over with no fewer than fourteen Neustadts!

To return to the question of the intrinsic importance of duplicated consonants in English literature—

THE DUPLICATION OF THE FINAL CONSONANTS IN ENGLISH WORDS BEFORE ADDING TO THEM A SUFFIX APPEARS TO FOLLOW NO KNOWN LAW.

Thus, for example, the final consonant is duplicated before adding the suffix, ing.

In Fit	—fit-ting,	but not in	Fix	—fix-ing.
,, Fan	—fan-ning,	,,	Fish	—fish-ing.
,, Dig	—dig-ging,	,,	Work	—work-ing.
,, Run	—run-ning,	,,	Stand	—stand-ing.
,, Flog	—flog-ging,	,,	Thrash	—thrash-ing.
,, Stop	—stop-ping,	,,	Stoop	—stoop-ing.
,, Begin	—begin-ning,	,,	End	—end-ing.
,, Slip	—slip-ping,	,,	Sling	—sling-ing.

Again, there are a number of monosyllabic words, such as—

Root —root-ing.
Reel —reel-ing.
Speed—speed-ing.
Sleep —sleep-ing.
Seed —seed-ing.
Weed—weed-ing.

In which the final consonant is not duplicated for an (imaginary) reason, once propounded to us by a philologist of some standing. His glibly-explained theory was that in all words with a terminal consonant preceded by a duplicated vowel, the pronunciation of the final consonant was so softened by the preceding vowels as to render its duplication, previous to adding the suffix, unnecessary. This euphonistic theory we had the hardihood, alas! at once to demolish by quoting to him a number of words in which no such euphonistic cause could be admitted to exist, and yet failed to find it necessary to duplicate their caudal consonants previously to adding the suffix, ing. Such, for example, as the harsh-sounding words —

Thrash—thrashing.
Stick —sticking.
Filch —filching.
Brush —brushing.
Work —working
Rend —rending, &c., &c.

In fact, it is a sad thing for the poor duplicated consonants which infest the English language, that the more minutely their case is inquired into, the more untenable is found to be their claim for conservation on philosophic principles. Their only *raison d'etre* appears to rest entirely upon the unstable and unsatisfactory shifting sands of the rule-of-thumb.

Let any one, for example, try logically to answer the question, "Why do we have a duplicate l in really, and n in sunny, and not a duplicate d in hardy, or a duplicate t in gouty?" Still more curious is the fact that when we turn the words sole and whole into adverbs we actually write them:—

Sole-ly —solely.
Whole-ly—wholly.

Again, let him attempt to solve the mystery on logical grounds, why the word puzzle is allowed to indulge itself in the luxury of possessing two z's, while poor hazard has to content itself with the possession of only one?

IT IS VERY DIFFICULT FOR A PERSON NOT SPECIALLY TRAINED IN THE ART OF MENTAL ANALYSIS TO APPREHEND THE ABSURDITIES EXISTING IN HIS MOTHER-TONGUE.

This arises from the fact that he is introduced to them in the nursery, before his brain has learned to think. He becomes familiarised with them at school, and they end by being indelibly grafted into his nature during his pupilage at college, so that by the time his reasoning faculties are fully developed he is no more conscious of their existence (unless his attention be specially drawn to them) than he is of the presence of a feather accidentally adhering to the back of his coat.

It is the foreigner who, with the greatest frequency and force, recognises the errors daily committed in a language. This is easily understood when we remember that very often he does not begin the study of the foreign tongue until his mind has been trained to think, compare, analyse, and generalise the materials placed at his disposal. It is for this reason that most of us so readily seize upon the weak points in the German, French, and other Continental languages, all of which possess within themselves a sufficiency of inconsistencies.

For example, upon what principle is a young German girl classed in the neuter gender—das Mädchen, a grown-up woman regarded as feminine—die Frau, while a wife is again reduced to the neuter gender—das Weib?

THE ENGLISH LANGUAGE IS SCARCELY ONE WHIT LESS ILLOGICAL THAN THE GERMAN.

While studying at Vienna, in 1854, we had this fact forcibly brought under our notice.

An Austrian gentleman, who was a fair English scholar, while reading an English book at the table where we were sitting writing a letter, suddenly threw down the book, and indignantly exclaimed, "Oh, de stoopid English, it eis unbearable." "What's wrong?" asked we in astonishment. "Wrong!—vi, everyding eis wrong. Here dis stoopid man tells de boys to stand fast, which means, I suppose, not to move. Den immediately afterwards, he tells dem to run fast, which is to move as quick as ever dey can. Oh! de stoopid! language for de same man runs fast, holds fast, breakfasts, eats fast, and yet fasts when he does not eat at all!!"

We smiled; but all that we could do was merely to retort that his language was not one whit less stupid than ours. Alas! two bads do not make one good.

Yet another objection may be offered to the abolition of duplicated consonants, on the ground that the spelling might not in all cases correspond to the pronunciation of the word.* This will, however, on investigation be found to be an invalid argument; for abundant evidence can be given that—

IN THE ENGLISH LANGUAGE THE ACTUAL SPELLING OF A WORD CANNOT ALWAYS BE TAKEN AS A CRITERION OF ITS PRONUNCIATION.

This may be illustrated by comparing the following words:—

Bough is pronounced like Bow.
Colonel ,, ,, Kurnel.
Corps ,, ,, Core.
Deign ,, ,, Dane.
Done ,, ,, Dun.
Hymn ,, ,, Him.
Quay ,, ,, Key.
Lynx ,, ,, Links.
Prophet ,, ,, Profit.
Red ,, ,, Read.
Thyme ,, ,, Time.
Ewes ,, ,, Use.
Mayor ,, ,, Mare.
Ewer ,, ,, Your.
Would ,, ,, Wood.

* Pronunciation is another word which "Time" has of itself lately shortened. It was formerly written pronounciation.

NOR CAN THE PRONUNCIATION OF AN ENGLISH WORD ALWAYS BE REGARDED AS A GUIDE TO ITS ORTHOGRAPHY.

Thus, we pronounce Ile and Iland, and yet spell them Isle and Island. It was not, however, always so. There was a time when Ile and Iland was considered the orthodox manner of spelling these two words; and so it remained, until some one, with a total disregard to euphony, introduced an s into them, and the public slavishly adopted the innovation, ignorantly supposing that the s was introduced on etymological grounds; the words having been derived (as they erroneously supposed) from the Latin word Insula—an Island. By placing the two words into juxta-position, however, it will readily be made apparent that such an impression is an erroneous one.

Thus INSULA has no similitude whatever to ISLAND (except it be in the number of its letters), either in its spelling or in its sound; while it is equally easy, on the other hand, to show that the original English word Iland came direct to us from the Teutonic stem, as both in the old Saxon word, Ealand, and the modern Dutch word, Eiland, we have the exact counterpart of our old English word Iland. The

English Spelling.

English Ile, again, is nothing more nor less than the non-modified French word Ile. Moreover, as the original pronunciation of the English words—Iland and Ile—is still adhered to, the sooner we drop out the mute, and consequently unnecessary s from these falsely spelt words—island and isle—the better will it be for the credit of our language and of our intelligence.

THE OMISSION OF DUPLICATED CONSONANTS— CONTRARY TO WHAT MIGHT AT FIRST BE SUPPOSED—WILL RARELY TEND TO INDUCE A CHANGE IN THE PRONUNCIATION OF THE WORDS FROM WHICH THEY ARE OMITTED.

At least it is not found that they have hitherto had this effect, and we can see no reason why they should do in the future what they have failed to do in the past. For example—

Shot { is still pronounced exactly in the same way as when it was written with duplicated consonants. } shott.

Dulness	,,	,,	,,	,,	dullness.
Fulfil	,,	,,	,,	,,	fullfill.
Peril	,,	,,	,,	,,	perill.
Wagon	,,	,,	,,	,,	waggon.
Man	,,	,,	,,	,,	mann.
Forest	,,	,,	,,	,,	forrest.
Bachelor	,,	,,	,,	,,	bacchelour.

And so on with many others, which it is

quite unnecessary for us to cite. In fact, in the vast majority of cases, it is neither the presence of, nor the absence of, a duplicated consonant which governs the pronunciation of the word, as is proved by the patent fact that words spelt alike are pronounced differently, while words spelt differently are oftentimes pronounced exactly alike.

It is the context alone which distinguishes the invalid gentleman from the invalid deed (which he unfortunately signed) when the word invalid is presented to the mind through the agency of the eye; and it is the context alone which distinguishes the mayor from the mare on which he rides when conveyed to the mind through the instrumentality of the organs of hearing.

So, in like manner, hopping and ridding will be distinguished from hoping and riding when they are shorn of their duplicated letters. The context will save them from ever being confounded with each other as easily as it saved the invalid and the mare from being confounded with the deed of the one and the rider of the other.

In fact, the further one investigates the question of English pronunciation, the less regard is ascertained to be paid to the mere spelling of the words. Ought, for example, for no apparent reason, is vocally sounded like nought; while light is entoned exactly like height.

We doubt not that there will be some few words from which the omission of a duplicated consonant will tend to render the spelling discordant to the pronunciation. Their numbers cannot, we imagine, possibly be great, as at the present moment we are acquainted with only one class in which this discordance is likely to occur. We allude to words containing a duplicated c; such, for example, as accident, success, and succeed. These, when written without the duplicated consonants, will read acident, succes, and suceed — an abnormality which is decidedly objectionable. Fortunately for our cause, however, the antagonism between the pronunciation and orthography is very easily removed, by the simple substitution of an x for the duplicated c. The words would then be written axident, suxes, and suxeed, and would not only offer no further impediment to our scheme, but have the additional advantage of being written in exact conformity to phonetic law.

Our pronunciation must be admitted to be perfectly arbitrary, and to follow no logical rule. Pronunciation, indeed, obeys alone the dictates of fashion. There is a fashion in language, even of the pulpit, as there is a fashion in the millinery of the stage.

The objection to the abolition of duplicated consonants on the grounds of their absence inducing an alteration in the pronunciation of the words from which they are omitted, is, therefore, as unworthy of acceptation as any theoretical over a practical objection can possibly be ; for the simple reason that very **MANY ENGLISH WORDS, ALTHOUGH SPELT DIFFERENTLY, AND POSSESSING ENTIRELY DIFFERENT MEANINGS, ARE NEVERTHELESS PRONOUNCED ABSOLUTELY ALIKE.**

Thus we pronounce

Abbé	like	abbey.	Altar	like	alter.
Boy	,,	buoy.	Bridal	,,	bridle.
Choler	,,	collar.	Lyre	,,	liar.
Feat	,,	feet.	Weak	,,	week.
Reign	,,	rain.	Aisle	,,	isle.
Hugh	,,	hew.	Ruff	,,	rough.
Knew	,,	new.	Blue	,,	blew.
Flour	,,	flower.	Our	,,	hour.
Air	,,	heir.	Eye	,,	I.
Bean	,,	bow.	Illicit	,,	Elicit.
Palate	,,	pallet.	Pair	,,	pear.
Bare	,,	bear.	Hair	,,	hare.
Beet	,,	beat.	Grate	,,	great.
Their	,,	there.	Two	,,	too and to.
Plain	,,	plane.	Here	,,	hear.
Need	,,	knead.	Deer	,,	dear.
Soul	,,	sole.	Doe	,,	dough.
Sun	,,	son.	Nun	,,	none.

There are, indeed, so many incongruities in

the spelling of the English language that one cannot help feeling that

THE IDEA OF MAKING ORTHOGRAPHY THE TOUCHSTONE OF AN ENGLISH EDUCATION IS FALLACIOUS.

Why do we write pull, and rule, when both are pronounced exactly alike? If there were logic in our language, we should be compelled to write them either as pull and rull, or as pule and rule.

Language, however, existed long before logic was born—long before grammar was thought of—long before the conception of a system of orthography entered into the mind of man. Language is itself an aged sire, while spelling is but one of its infant scions—not yet shorn of its swaddling clothes.

As in pleading a cause like this against two such potent enemies as Habit and Prejudice, it is essential, in order to have a chance of success, that every point in the argument should not only be so clearly stated, but so fully supported by fact, that it may at once appear to the mind of the reader as incontrovertible, it is requisite for us to make a slight digression for a moment from the point immediately under consideration, in order to dethrone two very common errors regarding the origin and growth of human speech; for a just appreciation of the true nature of language will exert a marked influence on the apparent plausibility of our scheme of literary reform.

AS REGARDS THE ORIGIN AND GROWTH OF SPEECH.

From the Bible telling us that our first parents were created in a perfect state, and in the image of their Creator, many good and worthy people have been led to suppose that Adam and Eve were, from the very first moment of their creation, in possession of a fully-developed language, and could communicate their ideas to each other through the instrumentality of vocal utterance with as much facility as any two educated persons can do at the present day. 'Tis hard for us to feel compelled to shatter into atoms this pleasing delusion; but stern truth brooks no restraint, and common sense, as well as philosophic logic, rebels against such a theory. The works of God surrounding us, beneath us, and above us, all plainly tell us that such an idea is an absurdity.

One might just as well say that God furnished our first parents with an alphabet, a grammar, a lexicon, pens, ink, and paper, as well as endowed them with a legible, bold hand of penmanship, in order that they might readily communicate with each other by letter.

We do not desire to wound the religious susceptibilities of any one particular class of our readers, but as honesty and truth are two of the most highly extolled attributes of man, we desire to place our views on the origin of speech clearly and fearlessly before our readers, without, however, running any risk of religious misconstruction. No one with the slightest pretence to education will surely venture to say that it in the slightest degree detracts from the power of the Almighty to opine that our first parents were created without the remotest knowledge of speech.

Adam and Eve were no doubt endowed by their Maker with the organs of voice; but the probabilities are that practice, and gradually developed experience, alone taught them how vocal utterance could be made subservient as a means of correctly transmitting thought. Like the language of the child not yet learned to speak, the language of our first parents must have been partially gesticular, partially vocal.

In the beginning human speech would be little elevated above a series of indefinite, spontaneous, clumsy ejaculations, and it would only be as pre-historic man slowly emerged from a rude state of being by the gradual natural evolution of his mental and physical powers, that his language, partaking of his general improvement, would become softened, more defined, and likewise more explicit.

We are naturally forced to this conclusion by the study of the remnants of articles indicative of pre-historic man's mode of life, which he has left behind him in his cave-dwellings, tombs, and kitchen middens.

By studying the nature of his tools, his weapons, his utensils, and his ornaments, we can form a pretty correct conception of what his occupations, his manners, and his tastes must have been at successive periods of his social history. And it is conclusively ascertained from these archaeological studies that man by slow and gradual stages emerged from a wild, rude state of being into a more, and more developed, and refined one.

Moreover, it will be subsequently shown that linguistic development follows the course of natural laws, in the wake of intellectual development, quite independently of the consort of any artificial purifying literary process.

It may here, perhaps, be as well to make the incidental observation that very many years ago it was suggested to us by a philologist of the highest standing—in fact, by the then President of the Philological Society—to publish our views on this very subject, and as a matter of fact the skeleton of this monograph was already sketched out for publication as early as the year 1859.

From the circumstance of our province being in the realms of science, and not in regions of literature, we, however, hesitated to send it to press, and in the end abandoned the idea of publishing it altogether, with the consolatory reflection that men's minds were not yet sufficiently ripe for the calm consideration the subject merited.

An important change has since then, however, taken place in the Anglo-Saxon mind. The ephemeral Spelling Bee unwittingly did a service (for which we cannot be too grateful) in successfully pointing out to reflecting minds very many inconsistencies; aye, it might even be said, many palpable absurdities in English orthography, while it had at the same time the advantage of conclusively proving that it is not necessarily the best educated persons who are the most proficient spellers. Thus it is that the paltry Spelling Bee, by prominently calling attention to these two important facts, set vibrating the chords of dissatisfaction with

English orthography in the educated, though somewhat indifferent breast; and it is chiefly owing to this latter circumstance, and the organisation of a Spelling Reform Congress, that this essay is now submitted to consideration, in the hope that ere the vibrating chords of dissatistion are permitted to regain a quiescent state, a decided, as well as a permanent improvement will be brought about in English orthography.

It may not here be out of place to make a few remarks on what is denominated

SPELLING POWER,

for it is pretty generally known that some men of high education and fair literary attainments can only trust themselves to spell correctly the ordinary words in everyday use, while many a man standing behind a shop counter, with no more education than what a parish school can afford, may spell correctly almost any word employed in the newspapers.

Many years ago our attention was forcibly called to a remarkable instance of spelling power, in the case of a little maid-of-all-work. It was related to us by a gentleman, when we were on a visit to the Lammermoor Hills, in 1848, and, as near as we can now recollect, he stated that while he was standing in the village "all-sort-shop," waiting to be served, he heard a lady customer tell the shopkeeper to address her parcel to so-and-so, and it would be called for. The shopkeeper bowed, the lady left the shop, and he began to address the parcel. He had not proceeded far, however, when he suddenly stopped, and, with a comical expression of countenance, put down the pen, took off his large round-eyed spectacles, rubbed them with the corner of his apron, and after giving to his whisker a twitch, replaced the spectacles on his nose, and took up his pen again. An intense stare at the parcel, a wise shake of the head, and a peculiar puckering of his mouth overcame the on-looker's politeness, and, with a quiet grin, he inquired of the shopkeeper what was the matter with him. "A weel, Sir, ye see I dinna ken hoo to spell that leddie's address. May be ye can spell it for me?" "Spell it!" exclaimed the stranger; "why, I don't believe that I could pronounce the jaw-breaking name. Is the place not in your own neighbourhood?" "Weel, Sir, it's certainly no far awa', only aboot five miles; but it's on the other side o' the hills, and oot o' oor district. I'll get Sally, and she'll spell it for me." Sally, the gentleman very naturally thought, would be an educated daughter of the shopkeeper;

but, to his surprise, on the name being called aloud, a dirty little slattern girl appeared, and stood in the doorway, between the shop and the back room, drying her wet arms with her ragged apron. She quickly spelt the word and disappeared. "Are you sure the girl has spelt the word correctly?" asked the stranger, on seeing the shopkeeper proceed to write it down. "I think so, Sir. Whenever the missus or me are no' shure aboot a word, we always ask Sally." "Has she been well educated, then?" "Not that I know of," replied the shopman. "I wish you would call her back, and let me ask her a few questions," said the gentleman. Sally was recalled, and the following conversation took place. "How old are you, Sally?" "Going thirteen, Sir." "Were you long at school?" "Not very; I left it at twelve, and came here to service." "How old were you when you went to school?" "I think I was about eight, Sir." "What school were you at?" "The parish school, Sir." Then, turning to the shopkeeper, the stranger asked if the schoolmaster was a clever man; and on hearing that he was nothing particular, he said to Sally, "How do you know how to spell that word?" "I read it on a cart one day." "Were you ever at the place?" "No, Sir." The gentleman copied down the word as Sally had spelt it, and subsequently found that the poor little ignorant maid-of-all-work had spelt correctly a word which defied his boasted learning.

If this story be correctly reported, it offers a nice puzzle for orthographists to unravel.

Much discussion has taken place regarding the peculiar nature of the spelling faculty. That the power of spelling does not altogether depend on education is now almost universally admitted. Moreover, that different degrees of spelling power are manifested in individuals of much the same educational acquirements and intelligence is a matter of everyday observation. It is well known that children of the same family, with about the same amount of mental power and training, spell with very different degrees of facility. Some people attribute this to a difference in ear, others to a difference in eye. Yet neither of these opinions is satisfactory, for no doubt, although the possession of a good musical ear is a great advantage, yet there are many deaf people who are excellent spellers; besides which, as we have seen, many words are not spelt as they are pronounced. The spelling power cannot, again, be said to rest entirely with the eye, for nearly-blind persons are sometimes fair spellers.

A third opinion is that the spelling faculty has but little to do either with the ear or with the eye, and that it entirely depends on a special faculty inherent in the brain, exactly as there exists in the brain an arithmetical faculty, quite independent of any special arithmetical training. To this third opinion we incline; for just as the arithmetical faculty is strongly manifested in some persons of moderate education, and of no very high order of intellect, so the spelling faculty is occasionally met with (as in the case of the little maid-of-all-work) in people with an equally moderate amount of intelligence and education.

It ought not to be forgotten, however, that much of the spelling power depends upon the possession of a good memory, and although memory is independent of a high order of intellect, a high order of intellect cannot bear fruit unless it is associated with a good memory.

So unsettled, even at the present day, is our English orthography, that in order to remedy the evils which still exist in having a variety of ways of writing the same word, it was a short time ago suggested at a meeting of the

London Association of Correctors of the Press to issue a "Printer's Dictionary" of all the words of disputed spelling, giving each word in one form only, according to the most general usage among the best standard writers of the present day. (Vide "The Publisher's Circular," Feb. 1st, 1877, p. 83.)

It ought not to be wondered at, then, that a knowledge of spelling has almost ceased among the educated class to be regarded as a trustworthy criterion of an Anglo-Saxon education. We believe that far greater confidence in judging of Anglo-Saxon education is to be placed on the construction of the person's sentences, than upon the mere spelling of the words.

It might be well for teachers of children always to remember, ere they punish a pupil for spelling wrongly, that the fault may not entirely lie on the side of the supposed delinquent, but depend in some measure upon an innate defect in the orthography of the word the pupil has been called upon to spell.

As regards pronunciation, again. Verily, of the variety of different modes of pronouncing the same word there is no end. Even at the present moment some of the most common of our words in everyday use have, at least, two equally correct (or incorrect) modes of pronunciation. Take the words either, and knowledge, for example. One set of people pronounce them in harmony with their true spelling, while another set of individuals, totally ignoring their spelling, pronounce them as ither and nolige.

DUPLICATED CONSONANTS OCCASIONALLY OCCUR WITH AMAZING FREQUENCY IN BUSINESS LETTERS.

With the view of illustrating this point the following has been composed, and it may be added, that although it consists of only one hundred and forty-six words, it nevertheless contains one hundred and two duplicated consonants, fifty-one of which, according to our rendering, are utterly unnecessary. It may be remarked, too, that no word possessing a duplicated consonant has been repeated, so that the letter cannot be said to present a sufficiently anomalous appearance to the eye, to attract special attention to its peculiarity.

Shipping Office, Millwall.

Sir,—I am sorry to have to tell you that the small case of Martells and Hennesseys' brandy, addressed to the committee of the —— Assurance Association, has arrived, with every one of its bottles broken. According to our commissioner's account (who happened to be passing the vessel when the accident occurred), it appears that there will be a difficulty in settling the question upon whom the loss of the goods ought to fall, for he says it might equally be attributed to one of two causes:—Firstly, the gross carelessness of the men engaged in unshipping the box; secondly, from the fact that, owing to some unaccountable reason or other, the words "Glass, with care," were omitted to be written upon it. The latter circumstance renders Mr. Cresswell, the shipper of the goods, liable, unless he can adduce sufficient evidence to attach the blame elsewhere.

The reason why so very few persons are aware of the extraordinary frequency with which duplicated consonants occur in the English language arises from the simple fact that the eye is so familiar with their appearance, that unless attention be specially called to them, they fail to attract notice. Now just as it is possible to write a letter full of duplicated consonants, it is equally easy to write one devoid of them, and yet use the words common in everyday life. A friend of ours, who takes an interest in this article, has written a paper entitled "Exhibiting Exotic Ferns,"* which consists of more than two thousand words, and yet contains only three in the possession of a duplicated consonant, and most unfortunately these three, as we are told, chanced to get into the article by mere oversight, or the paper would not have contained a vestige of one.

* T. M. Shuttleworth, Esq. "Journal of the Horticultural Society," January, 1877.

Nothing, perhaps, will impress more forcibly on the mind of the reader the advisability of getting rid of duplicated consonants than a glance at the post-office statistics.

We are informed by the annual report of the Postmaster-General that during 1875 more than one thousand millions of letters passed through the post-office, besides eighty-seven millions of post-cards, and nearly two hundred and eighty millions of books and newspapers. Will any one try to calculate how many millions upon millions of duplicated consonants this annual mass of correspondence represents, and then say that the abolition of them would not be attended with benefit?

Let us, for the sake of illustration, make a calculation of the duplicated consonants in the mere letters alone.

Four sides of a single sheet of note paper may be said to represent an average-sized letter, and on calculation it will be found that taking gentlemen's and ladies' letters together, the number of duplicated consonants in a sheet of note paper amount to about forty. Twenty of which are unnecessary. If so, a very easy multiplication sum will show that the corresponding part of the British nation writes TWENTY THOUSAND MILLIONS of unnecessary consonants in the brief space of a year.

While the millions upon millions of duplicated consonants occurring in printed books, newspapers, &c., continually passing through the post-office are simply incalculable; who, then, will gainsay that the abolition of unnecessary duplicated consonants from the English language will be unattended with advantages more than sufficient to counterbalance the trifling inconveniences attendant on the first introduction of the reform?

CERTAIN LETTERS OF THE ALPHABET OCCUR IN THE DUPLICATE CAPACITY WITH VERY MUCH GREATER FREQUENCY THAN OTHERS.

We have been at the trouble of counting the number of doubled letters in fifty thousand words taken from Lord Macaulay's "Critical and Historical Essays," two first-class novels, the *Times* and the *Standard* newspapers;* and we find that a duplicated consonant occurs on an average in every fifteen words, and that in every thousand duplicated consonants the different letters appear in the following proportions:—

* It is necessary to calculate the proportion of doubled consonants in writings on different topics, for on one and the same subject the same words are frequently repeated, and would, consequently, lead to error if the calculations were made upon them alone.

L	486
S	224
T	118
F	80
R	80
P	57
M	44
C	40
N	40
D	15
G	12
B	3
Z	1
Total double consonants	1,000

The four consonants, H, K, Q, and X, occur so very rarely doubled, that not one of them chanced to appear among the whole fifty thousand words examined.

The most frequently occurring letter of the alphabet, next to the consonants L and S, is the vowel E. E and O may be said to be the only two vowels that occur in a duplicate capacity, for A and I are exceedingly rare, while a doubled U is of course a thing unknown. The letter e occurs more than twice as often as the letter o, and their proportions to l and s are as follows:—

L	357
S	257
E	252
O	116
	1,000

As doubled vowels are necessary to indicate the proper pronunciation of words, with them we have no desire to interfere.

By natural evolution the language has already of its own accord got rid of nearly all the unnecessary vowels which were formerly so common in such words as

He	— hee.	Soil	— soile.
Be	— bee.	Down	— downe.
Do	— doe.	Room	— roome.
Air	— aire.	Mouth	— mouthe.
Been	— beene.	Four	— foure.
Begun	— begunne.	Year	— yeare.*

AS REGARDS THE ORTHOGRAPHY OF PROPER NAMES.

We beg to remark that as a man has a perfect right to call himself by what name he likes, he has an equal right to spell his name in whatever manner it suits his fancy. If the Woodds and the Forrests, the Abbotts and the Barretts, the Connells and the Donnells, the Hassells and the Riddells, the Ruffells and the Worrells, choose to write their names with double consonants, by all means let them do so. Personal names do not occur sufficiently often in writing to make the duplicated consonants in them a matter of inconvenience.

From the subjoined epigram it would seem,

* Vide Speed (1611), already cited.

however, that some persons, not content with merely doubling as many letters as they possibly can in their names, cause a little annoyance to their friends by attempting to double nearly everything else, and hence a Mr. Wellwoold had addressed to him by one of his especial friends these four sarcastic lines :—

> You double not only each story you tell,
> And double each sight that you see ;
> But you fill up your name with doubles as well,
> A double u, o, l, and d.

An equal fondness for the duplicating of letters in the name we perceive, in a volume lying on the table, is possessed by a Welshman, who writes his name as Llewellynn ; but whether this is done with the object of gratifying the organs of hearing or the organs of seeing, we are wholly at a loss to explain.

Even in the manner of spelling some Christian names there seems to be almost no end to the variety. The simple name of Theodore has been actually spelt in no fewer than sixty-five different ways. This may seem to be an impossibility, but a glance at the preface of Kingsley's " Roman and Teuton," page 17, will show it to be a fact, and facts, as we all know, are often stranger than fiction.

In some personal names there is an extraordinary frequency of consonants without the slightest attempt being made to double any of them. Thus, for example, we have been told by Mr. Vaux, Secretary to the Royal Asiatic Society, that there was formerly a watchmaker in Regent Street, whose name, which consisted of nine letters, possessed but one solitary vowel—an e. This curious name was "Wrentzsch." We cannot refrain from here briefly alluding to a spinster's idea of the personal disadvantage which might accrue to her by the abolition of duplicated consonants.

After having silently listened to our discussion of the subject with a learned brother of hers, she all at once exclaimed, "Oh, Dr. Harley, please do not try to do away with duplicated consonants, for if you succeed I shall for the remainder of my life be deprived of the only honorable title I ever possessed, and instead of being Miss, I shall be reduced to the level of Mis-understood." "Never fear," was our prompt reply, "though you should live to a hundred, you will never by any possibility be deprived of your honorable title by the abolition of duplicated consonants, for it is not in the caudal s, but in the capital M of the word the honor lies, and Mis (——) will be as much respected in the future as Miss

(——) has been in the past." Wonderful to relate, our spinster friend's fears were at once dispelled. This apparently imaginary dilemma of our spinster friend leads us to make a passing remark on an abbreviation in daily use— Messrs. for Gentlemen. It is, no doubt, a contraction of Messieurs—the French plural for Monsieur, which we have adopted as an English synonym; but why we have reduced it by only one-third (leaving six out of its original nine letters), when it might have been easily reduced by two-thirds, and still have been an equally good symbol for the term gentlemen, we are at a loss to understand. In addition to our theory of doing away with the duplicated consonant in the word Messrs., we would boldly venture to propose a still further shortening of the word by three more letters. Reducing it to Mes. to correspond with our abbreviations Mr. and Mrs. Only three out of the original nine letters would then be retained, and the contraction would really merit the name, and possess the advantages of an abbreviation. For the future we intend to write Mes. in our own correspondence, object to it who may.

Another friend, more interested in, and better acquainted with philology, one morning after we had been discussing the question of the abolition of duplicated consonants, sent to us by post the following witty lines :—

> "Oh! Doctor, listen to our prayers,
> All doubles don't suppress,
> Lest while you still retain our cares
> You leave us no caress."

The Doctor to the Canon in rejoinder :—

> "Ah! Canon, when WE once begin,
> YOUR occupation's gone.
> There'd be no use to preach 'gainst sin
> When sin *ners* there be none."*

Some sympathetic hearts might even object to the abolition of the duplicate s from caress, on grounds suggested to their minds by the pretty lines of the great George Canning, for as he says :—

> "A word there is of plural number,
> A foe to rest and peaceful slumber,
> Now, every word you choose to take
> By adding S you plural make.
> But if you add an S to this,
> Strange is the metamorphosis!
> Plural is plural now no more,
> And sweet what bitter was before."

To the poetic mind full license must be granted, but stubborn fact will soon show us that the bitters of care will never be confounded with the sweets of caress, even after the latter has been shorn of its terminal consonant.

* The Rev. Canon Tarver (Chester Cathedral).

The supposed confusion is based on theoretical grounds alone, and there never will, nor ever can exist any practical confusion in the employment of these two words, or even in the confounding of any other two words whose spellings are identical.

Paradoxical as this assertion at first sight appears to be, it is nevertheless quite as consonant with truth as was Columbus's assertion that he could make an egg stand upon its end. No sooner is the process made apparent than its paradoxical appearance vanishes, as we shall presently show at page 70.

Next as regards geographical and other proper names, we would make no exception in their favour, for the spelling of some of them, like that of Mississippi, is comical in the extreme. Would anyone, we ask, ever think of pronouncing Misisipi differently after the expurgation of its three unnecessary consonants? We think not. In proof of the assertion that

FOREIGNERS EXPERIENCE VERY GREAT DIFFICULTY IN SPELLING WHAT APPEARS TO BE SIMPLE ENGLISH NAMES,

we venture to call attention to a paragraph which fell under our notice in *The Mail*, of

27th September, 1876. It shows how an English word, apparently pronounced in an orthodox manner, may puzzle foreigners. The title given to the paragraph is, " A Polyglot Town ;" and it is therein stated that the Danish and Norwegian Consul at Ipswich has, for several years past, received letters from Northern Europe, on the envelopes of which are some extraordinary variations of the spelling of Ipswich. No fewer than 57 (!) incorrect spellings are given in the newspaper.

The only reason we can see for retaining so many incongruities in our language at the present time is that the schoolmaster is *not* yet abroad amongst us, and that we are incorrigible slaves to habit.

THE MOST POTENT OBJECTION THAT CAN BE RAISED AGAINST THE ABOLITION OF DUPLICATED CONSONANTS

appears to us to be the one already mentioned of its necessitating an increase in the number of words of different significations, with similar spellings ; and we are conscious that if we fail to clench this nail sufficiently firmly to prevent its being dislodged by irritable fingers, we shall be accused of having left a formidable objection obstructing the way to our proposed plan of reform. We will, therefore, add one or two still more conclusive arguments in its favour, and distinctly prove that the addition of a few more words of different significations, with similar spellings, is, in reality, only an imaginary obstacle in the path of the mode of literary reforms here suggested.

Attention has already been called to the fact that there is no difficulty in correctly interpreting the meaning of similarly sounding words, like flour and flower, eye and I, too and two, when they are presented to the "ear," although they have entirely similar sounds. We shall now proceed to prove that there cannot possibly exist any greater obstacle in correctly interpreting the meaning of words with different significations when they are presented to the "eye" with identical spellings :—

1st. For the obvious reason that it is not the ear that hears, nor the eye that sees, no more than it is the artificial tympanum inserted into the deaf man's ear, or the magnifying lenses in the spectacles of the short-sighted individual, by which the one hears and the other sees. The hearing and seeing part of the process is done, not by the artificial tympanum and lenses, but by the brain itself.

2nd. If the brain finds no difficulty in

interpreting differently-meaning words with identical sounds, it cannot have any greater difficulty in interpreting differently-meaning words with identical spellings.

3rd. In fact, it is neither the sound nor the sight of the word, *per se*, which indicates its true meaning, but, as before said, the context which precedes or follows it.

4th. Remove the context, and the brain would totally fail to appreciate the signification of the one word presented to it by the ear, just as much as it would fail to solve the meaning of the other word presented to it by the eye. It is the context alone which guides the brain to distinguish between soul and sole when conveyed to it by means of the ear, and it is the context alone which enables the brain to distinguish between slight (insult) and slight (slender) when presented to it by the eye.

5th. Therefore the reduction of a few more words, with different significations to the same spelling, can in no wise be regarded as a formidable obstacle to the abolition of duplicated consonants from the English language.

Since this article was written, we have perused an interesting paper on spelling in

"The Cornhill Magazine" for May, 1876, in which the author calls attention to the curious fact that Johnson spells

  Uphill with two l's, and Downhil with only one.
  Molehill ,, Dunghil ,,
  Illness ,, Talness ,,

There is, however, no necessity for us to go so far back as to the time of Johnson to discover inconsistencies in the spelling of our guide-books. Similar unaccountable inconsistencies are still indulged in at the present day. Turn, for example, to Dr. Hyde Clarke's "New and Comprehensive Dictionary of the English Language as Spoken and Written," and there it will be found that dullness is spelt with two l's, and fulness with only one. On what principle is this done? In the seventeenth century the words hill and well were generally spelt as hil and wel (*vide* Speed), and why an additional l was subsequently added to them, seeing that their pronunciation perfectly accorded with their spelling, it is difficult to understand, except from the fact that the benefits arising from the shortening of language were in those days neither understood nor appreciated.

 Enough has surely now been said to prove that the continuance of

THE EMPLOYMENT OF DUPLICATED CONSONANTS IN ENGLISH LITERATURE CANNOT BE LOGICALLY DEFENDED, EITHER ON PHILOSOPHICAL, OR ON PHILOLOGICAL GROUNDS,

nor on the grounds that their disuse will make the language less beautiful. Common sense, too, rebels against their retainment on economic principles.

With the abolition of duplicated consonants would be annihilated all the rules, with their fetters of exceptions, which so perplex our children, for the addition of a consonant here, and the subtraction of one there, in the formation of compound words, and their place would be occupied by the one single, great, and intelligible rule—namely, that

NO DUPLICATED CONSONANTS EXIST.

Life is too short, and money too precious, to be thrown away unnecessarily; and as the perfection of an art is to produce a maximum of profit, at a minimum cost of time and labor, perfection must be regarded as the goal of human progress, and philosophic simplification—the *ne plus ultra* of the age—the royal road thereto.

Why, then, should we hesitate to apply the process of simplification to the English language, and sweep from it, at once and for ever, many of the inconsistencies which at present hang around it?

By the abolition of duplicated consonants, as has been shown, we should but aid the efforts of "Old Father Time," who has long been silently engaged, and still is, and will ever continue to be engaged, in slowly lopping off with his pruning-hook all unnecessary vowels, as well as mute consonants.

LINGUISTIC ABBREVIATIONS.

Were we to take a still more minute retrospective survey of English linguistic evolution during the last three centuries, we could not fail to be forcibly struck with the remarkable abbreviation which has occurred during that time in a whole legion of the ordinary words in daily use.

As an illustration of the verity of this statement, we shall begin with the word bachelor. One hundred and fifty years ago it was almost universally written as bacchelour; so we see that it has lost two out of its original ten letters—a vowel and a consonant. Before the same period of time, ship was spelt shippe, and out of its six original letters it has lost two - again a vowel and a consonant. Sin was written sinne, so now only three out of its original five letters remain. A glance at the *Leisure Hour* for March, 1876 (already referred to), and at the page already cited, will reveal the words "soe suddayn, publick, and woeman;" while on the following page, in a letter headed "Trinity, Cambridge, October 31st, 1681," will be seen the words "lett slipp and physick," all of which have been shortened by "Time," without a single voice of complaint having been raised against the innovation, and every educated person has been a gainer thereby.

A saving of labor having been effected to the writer, to the printer, and to the reader, type has been saved, paper has been saved, ink has been saved, and it may be that an occasional fit of loss of temper has been saved to dubious spellers.

The natural process of national word-shortening can be illustrated in another way. Compare, for example, a German and an English sentence, the German being taken as the representative of an old language, the English of a new (and improved) one, and we shall soon discover how, by an unconscious process of natural national mental development, linguistic evolution has been compelled, by means invisible to our mental eyes, to economise our animal forces, in vocal utterance, as well as our manual labor in penmanship.

While the German requires twenty-seven letters of the alphabet to express the simple idea of

"Ich habe ein Aestchen zu spalten,"

an Englishman expresses exactly the same idea in seventeen letters—that is to say, with more than one-third less vital waste :

"I have a twig to split."*

After having given these illustrations, it is scarcely polite towards our Continental confrères to say—what is, nevertheless, perfectly true—that language is simplified in proportion to the mental capacity of its employer. The more muddle-headed the speaker, the more complicated, and, consequently, the more ambiguous is the language in which he expresses himself. The clearer the intellect, the fewer are the words it requires to employ in the transmission of its ideas ; just as the accomplished artist can in a few seconds, and with a few scratches of his pencil, delineate a facial expression, which it would take hours of time, and a multitude of strokes from the pencil of a second-rate artist to portray.

It is not alone the English language which shortens its words in the process of development ; all civilised languages, in a greater or a less degree, manifest a precisely similar tendency.

* See Whiting, "On the Growth of Language," p. 92.

The tendency to shorten words by dropping out letters from them is particularly observable when nations adopt words from each other's vocabularies. Thus, for example, we find that the Italians shortened the Latin word fides into fede. The French shortened the Italian fede into foi, while the Spanish reduced it into fe. So that at last fides lost more than one half of its original letters, notwithstanding which curtailment the word of two letters remained as potent a linguistic symbol of faith as ever ; for the Spanish word fe is just as powerful an expression of the conventional vocal sign for our word faith, as is the original Latin word fides, with its five letters. It is so exceedingly interesting to observe the linguistic alterations which words undergo in passing from one language to another, that we cannot refrain from subjoining the three following characteristic examples of the process, as seen in our English words, law, priest, and bishop.

1st.	Gothic	Lagyan.
	Saxon	Laga.
	Latin	Lex.
	English	Law.*
	French	Loi.

* We have occasionally spoken with persons who imagined that our English word law came to us from the Latin lex ; but the application of the phonetic test of derivation proves, on the contrary, that its original source is laga, be the derivation of the Latin word lex what it may.

2nd.	Greek	- - - -	Presbuteros.*
	Anglo-Saxon	- - -	Prysbeter.
	German	- - - -	Priester.
	Danish	- - - -	Prest.
	English	- - - -	Priest.
	Italian	- - - -	Prete.
3rd.	Greek	- - - -	Episkopos.
	German	- - - -	Bischof.
	Saxon	- - - -	Biscop.
	English	- - - -	Bishop.
	Portuguese	- - -	Bispo.
	Danish	- - - -	Bisp.†

Thus there is convincing proof that all European languages, as well as English, possess within themselves an inherent tendency to abbreviate the terms which they adopt from each other's vocabularies, and that, too, without paying any regard to the original form of spelling, beyond the retention of the minimum which is absolutely necessary to give phonetic expression of some part of the original sound.

No one need be the least surprised at this, when he recollects that words are merely conventional signs, and that no sooner has a new

* The word presbuteros is the ~~superlative~~ _comparative_ degree of comparison of the Greek adjective presbus, signifying old. Consequently presbuteros simply means the elder, an ecclesiastical appelation to an office-bearer in the church—in Scotland called an elder.

† Some languages, like the French and the Welsh, have changed almost everything about the original Greek word, except its primary letter, E; the French writing Evêque, and the Welsh Esgob.

word been incorporated into a language and become a recognised conventional sign of a given idea in the language which adopted it, than it may be said to be completely, and for ever severed from its parent stem, and made an independent entity, whose etymology henceforth dwindles down to be a matter of mere secondary importance to the language in which it has become naturalised. Just in precisely the same manner as a twig cut from a tree and planted in the ground becomes an independent tree. Throwing out its branches wherever it listeth, and blossoming, withering, and even dying independently of its parent. The bloom of the cutting may even in some cases cease to resemble in colour that of the parent plant. Thus the cutting of a red rose has been known to throw out a yellow bloom; and just like two straight lines once begun to diverge from a common point, the further they extend the greater becomes the distance between them, so it happens with words undergoing the process of linguistic evolution when engrafted into a new language. Moreover, it ought to be remembered that the shorter a word is made, so long as it adequately expresses the desired conception, the more pithy does it become. Dilution in every sense in language is a cause of weakness.

The exciting cause of abbreviation in language, of every kind, springs, no doubt, from an innate unconscious desire existing in the human heart to save trouble in transmitting to its destination the symbols of the idea it wishes to express. Not only the abbreviation of the adopted word, but the very fact of its adoption, proves this. Both the adoption and the abbreviation originate in one and the same cause, which may without injustice be said to represent a great principle in linguistic evolution — namely, the mundane desire to economise vital power in utterance, and manual labor in penmanship. Were it but possible for us to convey a complex idea to a listener by a single monosyllabic vocal effort, or to transmit a multitude of ideas to a reader by a single dash of the pen, language would then indeed be perfect ; but, alas! we are still far from that Utopian goal. Neither our powers of telegraphing the human voice,[*] nor our more complete modes of trans-

---

[*] Although the idea of transmitting sounds by electricity was put into a tangible shape by Reis in 1861, it is only now, sixteen years afterwards, that Mr. Elisha P. Gray has succeeded in transmitting the human voice with distinctness over a distance of 284 miles. The sounds are described as being as clear to the ear of the listener as if the speaker was but a few paces distant. The Telephone, as the instrument of communication has been named, is destined, without doubt, to produce a great revolution in telegraphy.

ferring thought to paper by means of shorthand, make beyond the very faintest approach to the great *ultima thule* of linguistic perfection.

The Spaniards have, as far as we are aware, outstripped all other nationalities in abbreviating language.

Like the French and the Italians, their tongue is of course merely modernised Latin, and we shall now further show that they have completely eclipsed their French and Italian *confrères* in shortening the original Latin words, as well as in making them more euphonious to the ear.

For example, instead of saying and writing

Oculus they say and write		ojo.
Mensis ,,	,,	mes.
Picis ,,	,,	pez.
Centum ..	.,	cien.
Milia ,,	.,	mil.
Video ,.	,,	veo.
Sapio ,,	,,	se.
Habeo ,,	,.	he.

And so on with hundreds of other words.

This abbreviation by the Spaniards, we imagine, is due to no other cause than that of saving trouble, for we know that the old Spanish proverb says, "Never try to do, what you can leave undone."

No one can dare blame the Spaniards for thus saving themselves time and trouble, for these are the two great objects of man's short life. What, forsooth, are all modern inventions devised for, but to save time and trouble? Why do our fair acquaintances purchase sewing machines, if it be not to economise time and labor, and thereby reap a corresponding advantage?

The Spaniards merit applause, not censure, for having adopted a simple and most efficacious means of not only saving themselves both time and trouble in speaking, writing, printing, and reading; but also for facilitating the acquirement of their language by foreigners, many of whom, like ourselves, are apt to grudge the waste of unnecessary labor in literary pursuits.

At an earlier stage of this monograph, it was promised that some farther facts would be offered in support of our views regarding the natural growth of language: and as this appears to be the proper place to introduce them, we shall begin by premising that we wish it to be thoroughly understood that no matter however much the pen and the printing press may have contributed to linguistic culture, the natural growth of all language uninterruptedly follows in the immediate wake of mental development, quite independently of the artificial influence of these two cultivating agents.

Had there never been an alphabet invented, either for the pen or for the press, the language of the Englishman of the nineteenth century, would still have shown a marked improvement over the language of his early ancestors.

The growth of language, like the growth of every other human attribute, is an inseparable concomitant of man's physical and mental evolution from a relative state of barbarism to a comparative condition of civilisation, quite irrespective of any of the physical methods which he may possess of transmitting thought, such as pen, press, picture, sculpture, monolith, chromlech, or cairn.

In illustration of the correctness of this assertion, we tabulate the eight following facts:

1st. It is in general conceded that pre-historic man gradually, and by slow degrees, emerged from a rude, rough, wild state of being, by a process of natural, physical, and mental evolution.

2nd. It has been conclusively shown by archæological research that the occupations, manners, and tastes of pre-historic men became in each succeeding generation more and more refined.

3rd. Written history proves that all languages, from as far back as there are any scriptory records whatever, have undergone very marked changes in their organisation.

4th. Every known language that has been reduced to writing shows a gradual tendency to become more powerful, and more exact, in direct proportion as the intellectual capacities of the individuals employing it become more developed.

5th. The more modern the language, the fewer are the words in it required to express any given idea.

6th. The more modern the language, the fewer are the number of letters of the alphabet employed in each word.

7th. The more modern the alphabet, the fewer, as a general rule, are its letters. For example, the Chinese, which is one of (if not) the most ancient of all languages, requires to employ many thousands of characters to explain its systems of ethics, philosophy, and science, which it takes from twenty to five-and-twenty years of a man's life to master. While modern English accomplishes the same task with six-and-twenty alphabetical characters, which any ordinary intellect can master in a forenoon.

8th. The more modern the language, the more euphonistic are the tones of its speech.

This statement can be rendered still more appreciable to the mind by simply tabulating some of the alphabets, and writing the number of letters in each opposite to it. Thus the

Sclavonian	contains	39	distinct letters.
Armenian	,,	38	,,
Iberian	,,	37	,,
Coptic	,,	31	,,
Persic	,,	30	,,
Arabic	,,	29	,,
Ethiopic	,,	26	,,
Gothic	,,	24	,,
Erse	,,	21	,,

The youngest of all, the Erse, as is seen, contains the smallest number. There is, however, a marked exception to this rule in the ancient Assyrian and the early Greek (a mere repetition of the Assyrian), which possess only 17 letters in their alphabets. But in spite of exceptions, the rule is seen by the above list to be, in the main, correctly stated.

As a necessary corollary to the preceding propositions, it may be said that the newer the language is, the more perfect is its organisation, orthography, and euphony. While it may be still further added—

A. That this is even the case where no distinct refining literary agents are discernible, except those spontaneously springing from the causes of natural linguistic evolution.

B. The more modern the form of speech, the greater is the brevity of its words and sentences, and consequently the greater is the saving of vital power in its oral and scriptory employment.

Such being the case, it is no exaggeration to say that the speech of the humble lowland Scottish peasant, which can scarcely be accused of having enjoyed the advantage of having had a literary nurse, as far as it goes, is a more perfect language than that used by the noble English peer in the House of Lords at Westminster. This assertion will probably startle many of our readers, and raise a smile of incredulity on the visages of not a few of them. However, we can easily prove that this is no exaggeration by applying to these two languages the crucial linguistic tests of euphony and brevity. Before doing so, however, let us remind some of our readers that although lowland Scotch is in common parlance designated a dialect, and dialect though no doubt it is, it is nevertheless a language in the philological sense of the word, quite as much as either Danish or Hollandish is; both of which are merely Teutonic dialects, though by usage and courtesy denominated languages.

A dialect is simply a limited language, or portion of a language, used either by an individual or a community, and all that it requires to constitute its right to the genuine title of language is an official recognition and employment in the affairs of the State, although it be neither printed nor written. The terms dialect and language are convertible into each other, according to their geographical distribution and mode of employment.

Some may be inclined to deny to lowland Scotch the title of a language, because it is only spoken by the common people, and is consequently vulgar. Beauty in anything, however, is only a fluctuating quantity, and just like right and wrong owes its significance to the merely arbitrary, temporary standard of a given time, which an equally artificial standard of another period may reverse, or even annihilate.

It is only necessary to cast a retrospective glance over past history in order to discover that what is considered as beautiful at one time is looked upon as ugly at another; what is regarded as right at one time is stigmatised as disgraceful at another; so that to say that Lowland Scotch is not a language, because at the present moment it is thought vulgar, and consequently ugly, is simply an absurdity.

We can easily make our meaning perfectly plain by relating the following anecdote:

In 1854, while standing in front of and admiring a picture of an ancient dame in hooped skirts, a young lady standing by our side exclaimed, "Did you ever see such a hideous dress? How could a woman with any pretentions to good taste ever dream of making herself into a guy like that?" Turning to our fair critic, we smilingly remarked, "Fashion is taste. Were hoops fashionable to-morrow you would immediately think them beautiful, and array yourself in the very largest of them." "No such thing, Dr. Harley; I never could admire a hideous dress like that, even were it the very tip-top of fashion." Strange to say, ere this same young lady was ten years older, we met her out at a grand ball given by one of our then ministers decked out in one of the most voluminous of crinolines we ever saw, and the good lady, now a matron, thought she looked magnificent in it. Her taste had changed with the fashion. Fashion was to her beauty. With this prologue we shall now proceed to convince our readers that the despised lowland Scotch dialect, patois, or whatever other name may be bestowed upon it, is not only more perfect in its organisation, but even more beautiful than high English. As we have just said, this can readily be proved by applying to the two languages the crucial linguistic tests of euphony and brevity.

1st. As regards euphony :

How much more harmonious to the refined ear are the words—

"Ye banks and braes o' bonnie Doon,"

than

"You banks and hillocks of pretty Doon."

2nd. As regards brevity :

While the English peer would tell his coachman to

"Drive slowly"—employing 11 letters of the alphabet, the humble Scotch peasant would say,

"Ca canie"—thereby employing only 7 letters to express exactly the same idea.

Again the English peer salutes his friend with,

"How are you all to-day!" (= 17 letters of the alphabet) while the illiterate Scotchman says,

"Hoo's a' we ye noo?" (= 12 letters of the alphabet) ;

Thereby making precisely the same salutation with an actual economy of nearly one-third of the vital power.

Lowland Scotch cannot, therefore, properly be said to be a despised language, on account of its organisation being less perfect than high English, but wholly and solely on account of its labouring under the misfortune of being an unfashionable dialect.

Were logic applied a little more assiduously to language than it is at present, some curious as well as startling linguistic revelations would be made.

As still further proof that we are correct in saying that the more modern, and consequently the more perfect, a language is, the greater is its brevity of expression, quite irrespective of any artificial literary culture, we shall pause for a moment and compare the modern Spanish with its elder sister French, and for the purposes of illustration, in order that there may be no mistaking our meaning, we shall select the very same sentences as we did in comparing low Scotch with English.

Thus, the Frenchman says to his servant,

"Allez doucement,"

while the Spaniard says to his servant,

"Vaya despacio."

So that while the Spaniard expresses himself in twelve letters of the alphabet, the Frenchman is compelled to use for the same purpose fourteen.

The shortening process is still more marked in the friendly salutation of,

"Comment vous portez vous aujourd'hui, Monsieur?"

in which the Frenchman employs no less than 39 letters of the alphabet, while the equally polite Spaniard, with his more perfect language, expresses precisely the same idea in 20 letters —nearly one half; for he simply says,

"Como está usted hoy, Señór?"

It is not to be expected, of course, that this shortening process is universally visible throughout the whole of these four languages. There are many exceptions to the rule; but if the languages be taken as a whole, especially as regards the social phrases in every day use, it will be at once seen that the newer the language, the greater is the vital economy employed in its utterance.

Of all the European languages and dialects which it has been either our pleasure or fate to hear spoken in the land of their nativity—and their number are not few, seeing that for no less a space than five years we wandered over the Continent of Europe, from Finland in the north, to Spain in the south, from Ireland in the west, to the Adriatic in the east—we feel ourselves compelled to say that the Welsh language—that of all others, the most highly extolled, as being the very essence of beauty by patriotic Welshmen—has appeared to us one of the least developed of all the European written languages.

In order that there may be no complaint raised against us by ultra-patriotic Cymerians, we shall apply to the language what we regard as the crucial linguistic tests of development— Brevity and Euphony —and in order that we may avoid being accused of partiality, we shall employ exactly the same form of test-agents as we have already done to the other languages similarly brought under consideration.

1st. As regards brevity in orthography.

Instead of employing, as in English,			The Welsh actually employ no less than		
3 letters to express Law			8 letters		cyfraith.
6	,,	,, Priest	9	,,	offeiriad.
8	,,	,, Holiness	14	,,	Sancteiddrwydd.
9	,,	,, Happiness	10	,,	dydwydduch.
10	,,	,, Excellency	16	,,	Ardderchowgrwydd.

These examples speak for themselves more strongly than any words of ours can, so we shall pass on without any further comment, except the passing remark that we know of no other language possessing a word approaching in the least degree in its orthographical construction to Ardderchowgrwydd, except that of the ancient British Druid, who gave to his Bachelor of Arts the distinguishing title of Disgibldisgybliaidd.

The modern, no more than the ancient Cymerian can, we fear, be accused either of brevity or of simplicity in his orthography. We shall now proceed a step further, and prove that, as a rule, he is equally guiltless of exhibiting any particular partiality for conciseness in expression. One single example will suffice for this purpose, if we select it from among the social phrases common in everyday life, and the most practical test with which we are acquainted is that furnished to us by compairing the universal form of everyday friendly salutation made by one individual to another.

The Englishman gives expression to his in 14 letters. } How are you, to-day?

Whereas the Welshman has actually to employ no less than 23 letters of the alphabet to deliver himself of the same polite question. } Pa sut yr ydych chwi heddyw?

The preceding examples (we could easily cite many more) are sufficient to show that, as a rule, not only are Welsh words longer, but at the same time more complex in their orthography than the English: and also that the

Welsh mode of expression entails upon the human vocal organs, in its utterance, an unnecessarily great amount of labor, while in writing it necessitates a needless waste of time and space.

2nd. As regards euphony.*

This is a subject that we must handle with great caution, otherwise we shall engender a flame of fury in many a patriotic breast. All Welshmen, without exception, that we have ever spoken to on the subject, and their name is legion, staunchly declare that their language is a most euphonious one, and they will no doubt consider that it is grossly maligned if we have the hardihood to opine that we consider their views on this point to be erroneous. As philology has no compunction of conscience in its linguistic criticism, in order to be impartial, we fear that, even at the risk of raising Cymerian ire, we must give a candid opinion, and state that to our ear, at least, Welsh, even when proceeding from the lips of a pretty Welshwoman, has never appeared to us particularly euphonious. In fact, it sounds to our ears not only inferior to Italian, and Spanish; but even to French.

---

* The euphony of a language is in a great measure proportionate to the number of vowels it contains.

This want of appreciation on our part of the beautiful Welsh language perhaps originates from the fact that we are not Welshmen, and, consequently, do not possess sufficient refinement of ear to enable us to appreciate its innate beauties, which are so apparent to the indigenous inhabitants of Wales.

With all due deference to higher authorities, we would further call attention to the fact that, in spite of the common Welsh argument that this language *must* be more euphonious than others, on account of the number of mutable consonants it contains, and of the y and w being employed as vowels, it seems to us that something must be radically wrong in it, or why should foreigners be always finding fault with it, and compel Welsh patriots to make such strenuous efforts to alter their opinions. The old proverb is, we fear, not altogether inapplicable here — "Good wine needs no bush."

We freely admit that we may be wrong; but, if we are to speak honestly, we must say that the results of the crucial tests of brevity and euphony when applied to modern Welsh prove that it is not only an immature, but an imperfectly organised language. This, to our minds, is very easily accounted for, on the ground that it is a very ancient language; for, paradoxical though it sounds, our linguistic investigations have led us to the conclusion that the younger the language is, so long as its foundation is built upon other languages, the more developed, and, as a matter of course, the more perfect is its organisation.

After the preceding rather severely-sounding critic upon Welsh, we must do it the justice of remarking that, antiquated though the language be, it nevertheless conforms to the linguistic law of abbreviating, as a rule, all the words which it engrafts from foreign tongues upon its own patriarchal stem. Thus we find it has shortened the spelling of the original words—

Dyans	(Sanskrit)	5 letters.	Dien	(French)	Duw	(Welsh)	3 letters
Canis	(Latin)	6 ,,	Chien	(,,)	Ci	(,,)	2 ,,
Cavallus	(Low Latin)	8 ,,	Cheval	(,,)	Cefel	(,,)	5 ,,
Episkopos	(Greek)	9 ,,	Evêque	(,,)	Esgob	(,,)	5 ,,

Numbers of other words might be added to these, which the Welsh language has of its own accord abbreviated. We must, however, admit that, on the whole, the proportional number is small when it is compared with that met with in more modern languages. For example, English abounds in abbreviations. It has shortened almost every word that it has adopted, and, what is still more, it has curtailed the orthography of even those from its own parent stem.

Thus, as an example, we may cite the following Teutonic words which have been abbreviated from

Königthum	into	our English	kingdom.
Weisheit	,,	,,	wisdom.
Irrthum	,,	,,	error.
Kommen	,,	,,	come.
Halten	,,	,,	hold.
Geben	,,	,,	give.
Haben	,,	,,	have.
Nicht	,,	,,	not.
Ochs	,,	,,	ox.

The English language has, moreover, not yet ceased in its career of linguistic abbreviation. It has, on the contrary, rather extended its sphere of action; and in obedience to an irresistible and definite law of linguistic continuity—after having passed through the first epoch of its development by attracting to itself a multitude of fragments from other languages—it has entered upon another phase of linguistic evolution, and now occupies itself in refining its collected materials, as well as in eliminating all extraneous and unnecessary cumbrous matter from them.

G

Not satisfied with only shortening the orthography of foreign words, as well as its own, it is now relentlessly engaged in abbreviating its phrases by applying to them another branch of the great natural law of evolutionary development.

The application of this branch of the great law is most particularly observable in the influence it exerts upon the colloquial English of the present day.

Within the last fifty years or so the amount of vocal and, consequently, vital power which has been economised is very considerable. And what is strange too, is, that this has actually been accomplished, in spite of the economising process having been almost universally (most erroneously) stigmatised as vulgarism. People forget that what is regarded as slang one day may be designated as classic English another. And so it is with vulgarisms; they are only vulgarisms until they come into general use—not after.

In illustration of the grounds upon which we found our assertion that the English language is still actively engaged in the process of saving time and labor in utterance and penmanship, we may cite the following colloquial phrases.

It was formerly the correct thing for a gentleman to say—

> I am going by the railway train.
> ,, ,, steamboat.
> ,, ,, omnibus.

Now he simply says (and it is equally correct)—

> I am going by rail.
> ,, ,, steamer.
> ,, ,, bus.

Again, in telegraphing to a friend, one used formerly to say, "Reply by telegraph;" but now he only says, "Wire reply."

In fact, the older one grows, the more concise and pithy his language becomes; and what holds good for the individual, holds equally good for the nation.

Our successors of 1,000 years hence will, we have no doubt, be able to express their ideas not only more lucidly, but a vast deal more concisely than we are able to do at the present time.

Having now redeemed the promise made at the outset, that every fact to be adduced in the chain of evidence for and against our plan of simplifying English literature, would be independently submitted to consideration, weighed, and appraised on its own individual merits, we feel ourselves, we think, in a position, from the data we have laid before our readers, to make the definitive assertion that there does not actually exist one single valid objection to our proposed plan of saving time and trouble in writing, printing, and reading the English language, by a total abolition of duplicated consonants from all words except personal names. We dare even venture to opine that there is only one potent obstacle looming in the path to the speedy success of the scheme, and that is the existence of our recognised national canker,

"PREJUDICE."

There are persons, we are aware, with temerity enough to assert that the organisation of the English language has become a fixation since the days of our great lexicographer Johnson ; and were this affirmation made by any other than a philologist, it would be deemed by us utterly unworthy of even a passing notice, for a more gratuitous assertion it is scarcely possible to imagine. Language, like human life in its passage from the cradle to the grave, knows of no period, no hour, no minute, when it can be logically said to be stationary.

Marvellous though the fact be, there is nothing in nature stationary ; and stranger is it still, that the laws governing the transition process are in themselves eternal, and immutable.

Uniformity and universality in their mode of application being at one and the same time the most characteristic features of these laws. The same law which causes the particle of dust to adhere to the sole of the boot, enables Mont Blanc to attach itself firmly to the surface of the globe; and the self-same laws which led to the organisation of the Anglo-Saxon language in early times regulate and control its evolution even now.

As in the physical world there is a definite law which compels two material bodies when they collide to change their physical form, so likewise in the philological world the same law compels two languages, or the parts of two languages, coming in contact with each other, to produce to a certain extent a change in the organisation of each.

The Anglo-Saxon, then, though it should continue to be a spoken language for a million of years, will ever remain transitory in its organisation. Like the flame of the gas-burner, its corporeal fixation is only an illusion, being nothing more than the evanescent representation of myriads of unseen infinitesimal linguistic particles undergoing in rhythmical sequence states of change.

As Heraclitus stated, "Life is nothing without movement," and it may now be added that nothing appertaining to life exists without motion, and consequently there is no language without change.

1st. In every civilised language, there are at one and the same time, a large number of words, only on trial. Introduced, but still not generally accepted.

2nd. There are also a number of old words slowly undergoing changes in their meaning, in their pronunciation, and in their orthography.

3rd. There are likewise a certain proportion of words slowly dying out, by a process of natural decay.

Consequently a man's vocabulary, even if there were no other causes at work than these, must of necessity gradually, though slowly, change from year to year.

To hesitate then to improve our language on the grounds of its fixation, would be little less illogical than to attempt to place a pyramid on its apex, instead of on its base.

Moreover, it is folly to say that Johnson, great lexicographer though he was, put an end to all linguistic change in the English language. A multitude of changes have already taken place in it since his days. Many of the words in general use in Johnson's time, have already actually disappeared from our spoken language altogether, while a host of other words that were utterly unknown to him, such for example as—

Skedaddle	Bezique
Crinoline	Guano
Benzole	Croquet
Paraffine	Lithium
Telegram	Flabbergast
Crohæmatin	Nitro-glycerine
Telephone	Spiflicate
Hæmin	Picaniny
Zanthin	Mythelated

and hundreds of others have glided in, and altered not only the quantity, but even the quality, of the language itself.

When any sudden general change has been proposed, such as that by Webster, of dropping out the u in all words ending in our, except Saviour, a furious outcry has been raised against the innovation; but after a time, the turmoil of hostility has subsided into the tranquility of calm acquiescence. We well remember the fate of the first article we wrote—for one of the Quarterly Reviews—according to Webster's system of orthography. When the proof sheets were returned to us for correction, every u that we had purposely omitted, had been carefully replaced. Whether at the suggestion of the then editor, or on the simple responsibility of the corrector of the press, we know not; for being at that time but a novice in literature, we deemed it inadvisable to rebel against the stern fiat, or even to inquire by whom the judgement had been passed. Years have slipped by since then, and now we find that when we indulge in the luxury of leaving out the letter u, the press sheets are returned to us with the same spelling as in the copy.

Even the sudden introduction of a new word into the language is sometimes sufficient to raise a storm of abuse from irritable pens. No one can have forgotten the literary hubbub which the introduction, a few years ago, of the word telegram occasioned. Nearly the whole daily press, led on (if we remember right) by a formidable leading article in *The Times*, denounced the innovation with torrents of invective. But like the fatal charge of Balaklava, "c'etait magnifique, mais ce n'etait pas la guerre!" The aggressors, in spite of all their dash and impetuosity, recoiled from the charge, themselves shattered to atoms; and now we see the word telegram daily raising its head triumphantly at the head of the column of "Latest News" in every newspaper in the land, *The Times* itself not excepted.

Although nothing can ever prevent fluctuations, both in the spelling and in the pronunciation, taking place in English words, we may safely prophesy that no such vast changes will ever again occur in any given future period of time as has taken place in the past, for there are now, as we already hinted, more potent conservative influences at work than ever previously existed.

1st. The great spread of common education is one.

2nd. The more general perusal of the daily press is another.

3rd. The easier means of locomotion by sea and land, tending as it does to retard the language from undergoing a rapid linguistic change, is a third ; while,

4th. The penny newspapers act as a great national linguistic conservative agent, for the four following reasons :—

A. Because all men, even the most learned in the nation, possess but a very limited vocabulary. In writing and in speaking they use over and over again the very same words, with only a sparing intermixture of different ones (when the subject is changed) to express a varied multitude of ideas. This fact was first prominently brought to our notice when attempting as a youth to read French novels. Every new author we took up compelled us, for the first forty pages or so, to have constant recourse to a dictionary, while long before we had finished his first volume we scarcely ever required to refer to a dictionary at all to understand his words; and we observed, too, that all the subsequent novels that were written by the same author were mastered by us, after our perusal of the first volume, with equal ease—that is to say, after we had surmounted the *pons asinorum* of the author's vocabulary; whereas the first volume of every new author taken up entailed upon us a greater or less amount of dictionary labour, until we had in a similar manner become familiar with the words our new author was in the habit of employing.

B. There is a great uniformity not only in the style of writing, but in the actual words employed by newspaper writers. Articles on the same subject in different papers, no matter how widely differing their views may be, are written in almost identical words.

C. The wide distribution of the penny press brings daily before the majority of the nation not only the same words and the same modes of expression, but even the same ideas. Hence the reader's views, modes of expression, and vocabulary of words, gradually become in some measure identical with those employed by the writers whose articles he is constantly in the habit of reading.

D. Had a daily press, such as we at present possess, existed in England in the days of Queen Elizabeth, and had it been uninterruptedly continued until now, much more of that Queen's English than we at present possess would have still remained in daily use.

Next to the penny press may be classed railways as the most important conservators of language, for the more the members of distant parts of the country are brought into oral communication with each other, the more closely will their dialects, and their words accord. This is easily proved by a glance at the great difference which now exists between the Dutch and the English languages which were at one time identical. They diverged from each other and grew into distinct languages only in consequence of the broad German Ocean interfering with the intimate intercommunication of these two branches of the Teutonic stem.

Even were we to separate a family of twelve persons, dwelling in the same house, into two halves, and allow no oral communication to take place between them, even though living under the same roof, in the course of a single generation there would already be observable a distinct dialectic difference in the members of the two sections of the family.

Before laying down the pen we would venture to remark that it ought to be impossible for any educated human mind, emancipated from the thraldom of prejudice, to regard otherwise than with pleasure a proposition which has for its object the facilitating the acquisition of knowledge, either by simplifying the means of its acquirement, or by removing obstacles from the paths of its transmission from one individual to another, through the intervention of apparatus, experiment, books, or lectures.

A man, therefore, who exerts his abilities to simplifying our means of transmitting thought, even should his efforts prove unavailing, should at least enjoy the privilege of obtaining an impartial hearing. Every educated Englishman owes a deep debt of gratitude to our American collaborator, Noah Webster, for the strenuous efforts he made to shorten, and to simplify, our imperfect language; and it is much to be deplored that his endeavours met with such scanty support—even equivocal approbation—on this side of the Atlantic. Many of the literary class acted like short-sighted and prejudiced individuals; and instead of marshaling themselves in the van, and granting him their support, as they ought to have done, lagged behind, and reluctantly allowed themselves to be dragged along in the rear.

It is strange that though literary men are, as a class, the most enlightened on things in general, in too many instances they are totally ignorant of, or at least unmoved by, the blurs and blemishes upon things immediately appertaining to themselves.

If, for example, a perfect stranger to them, as a class, was to form his opinion of their mental calibre, solely from what is generally known regarding their luke-warmness in the regeneration of the vocal and manual means for transmitting thought, he would be compelled to rank them, as a class, among the narrow-minded members of the community; there are so many among them who appear entirely to forget that speech and writing have absolutely but one object in view, namely, to serve as a ready means of mental intercommunication.

Every superfluous word, every superfluous syllable—even every superfluous letter in a word, being an actual disadvantage to the recipients, as well as to the distributors of thought. In a language, dilution in every sense, as before said, is a sign of weakness; so that every means which tends towards linguistic abbreviation should be welcomed as an addition of strength, instead of its being received—as it now too frequently is—with a cold shoulder.

Would not this stubbornness be less apparent if they would condescend to write the word without its three unnecessary duplicated letters b, n, and s?

Before saying adieu to our subject, we would beg to call attention to the fact that we are by no means the only persons who have endeavoured to obtain a diminution of the number of duplicated consonants in the English language; and although nothing has come of it hitherto, we will venture to prophecy that, sooner or later, duplicated consonants are doomed to disappear *in toto* from our literature. The natural evolution of the language itself demands it; and in asking our contemporaries to lend a helping hand to the overthrow of duplicated consonants, we are but asking them to aid in hastening an inevitable result, which will of itself follow, as a natural sequence, upon the more complete development of the language.

Unfortunately, all philologists are not philosophic linguists, and, consequently, they are occasionally found straining at gnats while they swallow camels! It is, therefore, not impossible that our plan of saving time and trouble in English literature by the abolition of the unnecessary duplicated consonants may encounter opposition from a few of them. For it is a pitiable fact that, however numerous may be the liberal-minded who are ready and willing to acknowledge the merits, and put into practice the advantages, of a new scheme, there are always a much larger percentage of narrow-minded individuals eager to point out its defects and to impede its progress.

Human nature is so fond of airing its real (or its imaginary) wisdom, that it never fails to let slip the opportunity of magnifying a deficiency of wisdom in its fellows; so that, even in cases where the merits of a new device are in greater proportion than its defects, the former are apt to be passed over with scanty recognition, while the latter are vauntingly paraded before the eye of the public, and gloated over by the would-be supposed-to-be impartial critic. Too true it is that all men are wise in their own conceit.

Be the supposed objections to the present scheme what they may, it must at least, we think, be conceded by all who give a careful perusal to thse pages that there are no difficulties in the path to the practical adoption of this improvement in English orthography, such as those which so unfortunately beset the way to the speedy introduction of phonetic spelling, which is so desirable.*

The goal before us is not only one of easy accomplishment, but the prospect in sight is one of universal and permanent advantage.

Even admitting that the change will for a time be associated with some trifling inconvenience, surely such a consideration cannot weigh heavily in the balance against its adoption, since the inconvenience can only be temporary, while the resulting benefits will endure for all time.

Without diverging from an already existing custom, no progress whatever towards perfection in anything is possible, and it is only by

* Who among us would think his photo any less charming because it was spelt foto ?

disregarding existing rules that new and improved methods are developed ; just as it is necessary for the assayist to begin by destroying the mineral, in order to be able to extract from it the pure gold.

It is not improbable that the suggestion of the abolition of duplicated consonants is before its time, and will, therefore, perhaps meet with the approval of but a few of the more advanced philologists, while a storm of invective is raised against it, and cause it to appear as if about to be totally overwhelmed in the surf. The raging billows will probably, however, pass over it, and in the quiet water behind, it will raise its head triumphantly : for being founded upon the principle of Simplification—the life-buoy of improvement in this progressive age—and having for its sheet-anchor the saving of Time and Labor, it is impossible for it, we think, to be permanently swamped, no matter how long or how fiercely the stormy billows of prejudice may rage around it.

Since it has been clearly shown that the abolition of duplicated consonants from English literature will be an unsullied gain to every man, woman, and child reading and writing the language—be they natives or be they foreigners—we may now ask, " Wherefore should we refrain from doing at once, and for all time, that which must inevitably, after a lapse of years, take place, by the hands of Nature's Great Reformer?"

Faint-hearted philologists may utter their wailings of regret over this orthographical change in English literature; but while so doing, let them pluck a twig from the tree of comfort, and console themselves with the reflection that, by the abolition of duplicated consonants, there is no fear that their beautiful language will suffer shipwreck on the

ROCK OF COMMON SENSE.

Before bidding a final adieu to our subject, we ought not to omit to mention that we have had a more ambitious aim in writing this monograph than a mere desire to save Time and Trouble in the Writing, Printing, and Reading of the English Language. Our real object has been to call the attention of all educated men, in every quarter of the globe, to a class of general principles which, when properly applied, cannot fail to ensure the simplification of all languages already reduced to writing, or which yet remain to be enrolled in the general economy of literature.

If our scheme of simplifying English literature should meet with public approval, and be successfully introduced, we incline to believe that its visible advantages will be so great that other nationalities will very soon be tempted to enter their languages upon the same course of literary reform. The French and the German—indeed, every language—cannot fail to be benefited by pursuing the course of procedure we have indicated, and we imagine that generation upon generation, yet unborn, will find cause to rejoice at the wisdom of their respective forefathers, in the last quarter of the nineteenth century, for having saved them from an immense loss of vital force in literary labor.

Having now fairly launched our little bark on the restless and endless ocean of thought, we leave it to the tender mercies of the winds and waves of Public Opinion.